CHANGING THE WAY YOU CHANGE

2nd Edition

VANESSA BRIDGES, PH.D.

This book was written in good faith and is a work of non-fiction. It provides information based on the author's education and opinions in psychology, theology, biology, and physiology. As newer research is being revealed, the author and the publisher make no explicit guarantees as to the accuracy of the information contained in this book. The concepts used are the essential aspects of this writer's message to encourage you to begin a self-evaluation for a deeper conversation with God in your holy place.

Copyright © 2016 by Vanessa Bridges

Second Edition: © 2024

ISBN: 979-8-9922034-0-0

Original copy editing by Gary Sciascia

2nd copy editing by Greg Jonason, PH.D.

Book designed by Mark Karis

All Scripture quotations, unless otherwise indicated, are taken from the Holy Bible, New International Version, Copyright 1978, 1986, 2011, by International Bible Society.

For more information or to book an event, contact: ctwyc.book@gmail.com

Printed in the United States of America

CONTENTS

PROLOGUE

The Bible states you are "fearfully and wonderfully made" (Psalm 139:14). The "you" God created is His gift to you, and as such, He has endowed each of His "fearfully and wonderfully" made creations with God-given potential. God entrusted you with His image, which grants you the capacity to have a relationship with Him. A relationship with God allows you to develop an unselfish, loving persona that honors Him as Lord by your behavior, attitude, and willingness to change those things that have negatively influenced you in this world. However, to realize that enormous potential, you must accept and appreciate His gift, then use and share it. How you use this gift is up to you. *Changing the Way You Change* is not necessarily advocating that you give up what you have learned to care about, but that you better manage those things you care about to His glory. *"We proclaim Him, admonishing and teaching everyone with all wisdom, so that we may present everyone perfect in Christ. To this end I labor, struggling with all His energy, which so powerfully works in me"* (Colossians 1:28-29).

"Those who oppose Him he must gently instruct, in the hope that God will grant them repentance leading them to a knowledge of the truth" (2 Timothy 2:25). My prayer is for you to begin a life-changing conversation with God that will align you more thoroughly with His plan for the rest of your life. Once we learn how to live in the freedom of Christ, our worship (reverence) of Him will be one of obedience. In order to get better at something, we must put it into practice. So, changing will require you to take a candid and intimate internal look at "you" in a maladjusted S.E.L.F (Self-Evaluation Leading to Freedom) while maneuvering through this world.

INTRODUCTION

Although you might find some change difficult, rest assured that it is possible as you increase your understanding of God and your willingness to change. *Changing the Way You Change* helps clear your mind to pursue who you were created to be. This book provides personal and practical information to move you to receive the life God is offering. *"To man belong the plans of the heart, but from the Lord comes the proper answer of the tongue. All a man's ways seem innocent to him, but motives are weighed by the Lord"* (Proverbs 16:1-2). *"The mind of sinful man is death, but the mind controlled by the Spirit is life and peace... It does not submit to God's law, nor can it do so. Those controlled by the sinful nature cannot please God."* (Romans 8:6-8). The concepts herein are biblically driven and grounded in God's truth.

Dr. Sylvester Outley, my mentor, believed that the human mind still holds an ancient orientation of superstitions and savagery developed over a millennium of improper and unethical human conditioning. Dr. Outley was optimistic that his mind and belief system were contaminated with untold years of negative attachments to this physical world. These attachments opposed his spiritual life. Contrary to God's principles, his true faith was subconsciously in people, places, and things in the physical world. As many of us sometimes do, Dr. Outley was talking about faith but not sincerely walking the walk. You will take the "dys" out of your dysfunctional life when you change God's way. We must stop listening to our unrenewed minds and its logic. We will make great progress when we give God all our childish attitudes by developing the art of discernment (the ability to make judgments based on spiritual guidance and understanding). *"Do not conform any longer to the pattern of this world, but be transformed by the renewing of your mind."* (Romans 12:2). *"Blessed is the man who finds wisdom, the man who gains understanding..."* (Proverbs 3:13).

In the words of William Booth, founder of the Salvation Army (1829-1912): The chief dangers confronting the coming century will be religion without the Holy Spirit, Christianity without Christ, forgiveness without repentance, and salvation without regeneration. The greatness of man's power is the measure of his surrender.

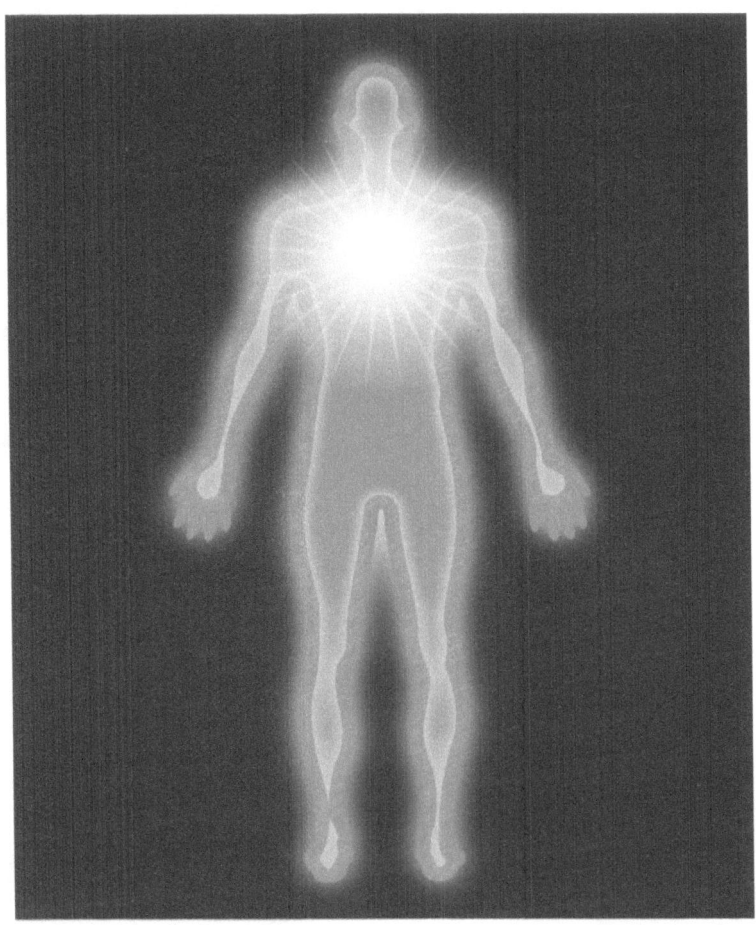

The Triune Being—Our trinity—body, soul, and spirit

1

METANOIA

(Greek word for a change of mind)

"What has been will be again, what has been done will be done again; there is nothing new under the sun" (Ecclesiastes 1:9). Or, as we might say today, there is nothing new, only repackaged. Only our perceptions make things unique by modifying how something is packaged and used. Accordingly, the internal mindset of humankind has not changed since creation; only the technology we use to satisfy ourselves has changed. Humans still have the exact emotional and physical needs we had from the beginning. We still have the same insecurities, questions, and fears about life. We still take our eyes off God to do things our way. Our internal growth has often stagnated because we are too focused on meeting physical needs at the expense of an inner transformation.

The Bible provides information on better managing our trinity (body, soul, and spirit) for internal growth. Still, most of us continue to hang on to perceptions and beliefs learned early in our lives without spiritual validation or truth. Our memories and experiences contributed to our beliefs (see Chapter 3, 'Understanding You'). We are unaware of how our thoughts and emotions are expressed in the body. To illustrate this point, take the word "meek," which Jesus used in the sermon on the mount in Matthew 5:5, when He said, *"Blessed are the meek."* Today, we associate meekness with weakness. However, a more biblically accurate definition implies not only a gentle nature but obedience to the Lord; therefore, teachability. Surrendering your will to God takes great inner strength (meekness). Learn to bear sufferings in patience and meekness because nothing is as important as the humbleness of heart and detachment from your own worldly opinion and will. Meekness is nothing more than strength under control.

"In the past God overlooked such ignorance, but now he commands all people everywhere to repent" (Acts 17:30). Metanoia is God's design for change that purifies how we think, which determines how we act. This purification is a cleansing that can only be initiated from repentance with a spiritual conversion that leads to salvation and leaves no regret. It is a transformative change of your soul that improves your mental perspective. *Changing the Way You Change* must start with recognizing and assessing your fears, internal philosophy, core beliefs, and perceptions. Once evaluated, you can be released from shame, regret, guilt, and doubt associated with past wrongs and the wrongs done to you. *"Godly sorrow brings repentance that leads to salvation and leaves no regret..."* (2 Corinthians 7:10). So, your active willingness to change demonstrates a personal commitment to living for Christ daily.

"...If I am telling the truth, why don't you believe me? He who belongs to God hears what God says..." (John 8:46-47). My life

experiences have governed my thinking and how I live. At times in my life, embarking on specific aspects of self-improvement was difficult and even frightening. But the change was unavoidable. I consumed numerous self-help books and read research studies stating few substantive differences between how Christians lived and the general population. So, as a baby Christian, when I initiated changes in my life, I was prone to imagine how easy the apostles had it. After all, they had Jesus in the flesh to redirect them by confronting their faulty thinking and ungodly behaviors. But my lack of discernment kept me from experiencing God intimately as I focused on things outside myself. I was worshiping God based on how other people were worshiping Him. I found myself a new Christian with no grasp of how to change. I was trying to adjust Christianity to my upbringing and all my former experiences. Therefore, I could not comprehend how worldly standards influenced my perspective on God's Word. I became disillusioned in my walk with God as my environment and circumstances overly influenced me. Satan's taunting soon overpowered me as he waged war on my internal skills and left me distanced from God.

Although my education prompted me to look deeper within to discover myself, this proved to be ineffective in changing me internally. My critical thinking skills were colored with clouded filters as the information I took was stored. I never grasped at a core level how to differentiate between opinions, insinuations, truths, and facts, nor could I reflect on their reliability. I could not account for my biases and how they shaped my worldview. I became stuck in a rut as I fought my internal battles using earthly wisdom, education, and logic. I had not yet understood how Christ could prompt a new life in me. I did not believe or accept God's truth at my core level.

CHANGING THE WAY YOU CHANGE

As I struggled to understand how the power of Jesus' blood allowed me to enter God's presence, I grew weary in my efforts to change as I misunderstood God's plan for growth. I could not see the stubborn and hidden holds I had over my life. Nor did I know how to work through my internal pains and emotional issues. The temple God created within me to house His Spirit had become unsafe. I was emotionally depleted, unable to take a mental break from my pain. My heart had become empty as I re-experienced transgressions in my life. I could not disconnect emotionally from what I felt the world owed me for my miseries and hurts. So that you know, the unregenerate human sometimes loves their sin and continues to battle with it even after conversion. So, I continued to rely on my worldly perspectives to understand God's message. I did what I was advised: the bare minimum of the Christian life: praying, reading, serving, repenting, and forgiving. But to be honest, it was just a series of external exercises I did as my internal turmoil continued. I never grasped how to uncover my identity in God for true repentance, nor what He created for me to do with my life. *"... I do not understand what I do. For what I want to do I do not do, but what I hate I do... I know that nothing good lives in me, that is, in my sinful nature. For I have the desire to do what is good, but I cannot carry it out... When I want to do good, evil is right there with me. For in my inner being I delight in God's law; but I see another law at work in the members of my body, waging war against the law of my mind and making me a prisoner of the law of sin at work within me. What a wretched man I am!"* (Romans 7:15-24).

During my self-evaluation, a few scales dropped from my eyes, and it became apparent that my struggles were within me. I was blessed to realize the primary issues in my life were not circumstances or other people who hurt me—my real enemy was my thinking process. I then understood that my mood was a by-product of my behavior and experiences that profoundly impacted my perspective. Through prayer and reflection, I was blessed to uncover my faulty perceptions. I was enlightened to see a slight advantage over the apostles in changing, even though I did not exercise it properly. I have God's Word and laws in my heart and in written form for daily reference. Although I have always had instant access to His Word, my internal obedience was lacking. His written words are the seed planted in our spirit so we can grow each time we read, hear, and act upon it. As I gave God's Word authority over my life, it meant giving up, or at least tapering my free will desires and redirecting them toward glorifying God. *"...I will put my law in their minds and write it on their hearts. I will be their God, and they will be my people. No longer will a man teach his neighbor...because they will all know me, from the least of them to the greatest..."* (Jeremiah 31:33-34; Hebrews 8:10-11). My prayer to God: that He loves Himself inside of me. Before going further, let me share my internal need to change more in-depth. It began with one of the darkest moments in my life. Many things happened that should have prompted me to change, but one event shocked me to the core. My younger sister decided she could not deal with life and committed suicide. My two small children and I were the only ones home then, and I was immediately thrown into a black hole with no means of escape. It held me down physically and mentally as it sucked the life out of me.

I went through mental and emotional breakdowns as I could not feel anything. Metaphorically, I could see and feel its presence, but could not extract myself from its grip. I only sensed people's presence as faceless shadows. For years, I isolated myself in a pit of self-pity. Each day was unrecognizable and unmemorable. Her act of suicide was too much for me to accept. I got angrier at the world and everyone in it. My anger made me feel like I did not deserve to be happy, nor did anyone else. Nothing gave me pleasure or comfort; even other people's laughter evoked angry feelings within me.

"When I said, "My foot is slipping," your love, O Lord, supported me. When anxiety was great within me, your consolation brought joy to my soul" (Psalm 94:18-19). No matter what I did, I could not shake the impact of her decision. Because I was mentally and emotionally exhausted, I did not know what was real! So, memories of my sister hovered over my home and fueled my negative thoughts. She rarely left my thoughts and even plagued my nightmares. As a result, I was tossed about, unsure of which direction my life should take. The proficiencies I had at that time were ineffective in managing my emotions. So, Satan used guilt and shame to keep me attached to her in an unhealthy manner. I was powerless against his destructive tactics because I had not mastered the skills to challenge his lies. Satan's insinuations twisted my inner thoughts and core beliefs. He wanted me to sit and be lonely, angry, self-absorbed, untrusting, and critical. As my faulty thoughts strengthened, I did not know how to get my "self" out of the way. So, fear fostered negativity and biases, which became my constant companions. This emotional burden became the ammunition that fueled my own suicidal thoughts. I often prayed for God to take my life because I was too afraid to do it myself.

Even with two small children to care for, I was ready to give up on life. Her death was the catalyst that made it easy to give in to my selfish and negative mindset. I had become a walking and breathing zombie of sorts. My hair fell out in clumps as I barely rose each day to dress and shower. My family and friends had no remedy for me. I was finally given (not prescribed) medications, prayed over, given scriptures to read, and then left alone to be consoled by my beliefs and negative thoughts. I doubted what God would or could do for me, as I kept my suicide option open.

"The thief comes only to steal and kill and destroy; I have come that they may have life and have it to the full." (John 10:10). I became so overwhelmed with my thoughts that each time I got into my car, I imagined how easy it would be to drive the vehicle off the highway or bridge. My hands would lock onto the steering wheel as tears raced down my face. "What are you waiting for? This can lead to your death. Go ahead and do it," I thought to myself. With a slight turn of the wheel, I could feel the heaviness of the car's movement, which would cause other thoughts to rush in, "Don't be so unwise; if you do this, it might not work, and you could be left in a vegetative state; then your life would be worse than it is already." This possibility frightened and deterred me. So, I stubbornly sat back and accepted my current path of self-destruction by doing nothing and being miserable. As you may know, stubborn people always believe their actions (or inactions) are correct. The chilling part is that I continued to defend and justify my thoughts of wanting to die. Hence, my warped thinking included ideas like, "I am not afraid of dying—I do want to die, but there is a better method. What if I survived with a dysfunctional body and would not have the opportunity to try again!" As I continued to justify my thoughts, I held fast to the perspective that I was in control and simply planning a better way.

Consciously, I had never recognized fear as one of my character flaws. Fear has strong components such as doubt, anxiety, procrastination, criticalness, insecurities, and fright. The opposite of fear is curiosity, trust, courage, and calmness. None of these qualities described me internally. Growing up with six siblings, I developed ways of behaving that camouflaged those aspects of fear. So, over the years, I appeared fearless and confident. As I tried to change to escape my prison, the heavy weight of anger kept my mind and body doing the opposite of what I desired them to do. As it turns out, many emotions like anger, anxiety, and depression are similar, although they may have different behavioral manifestations. Each can evolve into the other if not dealt with appropriately. My intense grief and fear dominated my thoughts, leading to internal dissatisfaction, shame, regret, and entitlement issues. As a result, my first impulse was to mistrust. This was demonstrated outwardly by misreading or attacking the intent from any perceived source, be it a person, object, or situation. To lessen my internal pain, I did what I did best: I put more trust into my dysfunctional beliefs to navigate through life.

As the battle continued within me, it was difficult for me to see how my maladaptive ways had manifested themselves throughout my life. I was also unable to take control of my thinking, so my ungodly mind took control of me. As a baby Christian, it was even more challenging to differentiate between my unspoken prejudices and my foundation in Christ. From our youth, most of us need to be equipped to distinguish facts from opinions from truths. It is easier for us to think about how we were culturally trained to believe, give in to what feels right, and be driven by our emotions. But our emotions lack the spiritual substance from God's truth. The consequence of that laziness is the inability to bring your body into harmony to receive God's plan for salvation. Frank Outlaw summed it up best in his poem, "Your thoughts become your words; your words become actions; your actions become habits; your habits become a character, and your character becomes your destiny."

My body had gotten so used to being depressed and miserable that it continued producing a volatile chemical mixture. I had become comfortable in that miserable state because it was easy (a no-brainer). My cortisol levels were extremely high, so I was mentally and physically incapable of getting through this transition with sheer grit. Getting my body to produce pleasure chemicals like dopamine, serotonin, and norepinephrine in harmony would take some internal work. From my core, I had to change my beliefs, behaviors, thinking, and attitude. I had to surrender my faulty core beliefs and negative thinking to adopt a healthier mindset. Being fully aware that one cannot be sad and happy at the same time, I had to make a choice to blindly trust God, even in my pain and misery. I had to release my established personal rules that blinded me to my character flaws. During my self-assessment, I also grasped that I had been living on the sidelines of life and not participating in God's miracles or His grace. So, I had to wrestle with who God had created me to be by developing an appreciation for my life, scars and all. I could see, by His grace, just how far I had fallen. I had been living on the porch of His temple and assumed I was inside the temple with Him.

Although I believed in Jesus Christ from an immature age, I did not have the spiritual nutrients to sustain a growing faith. But no matter how tiny that mustard seed of faith was, it deterred me long enough to change my destructive path to develop a more intimate relationship with Him. To find a way to change, I began to meditate and read the Bible from cover to cover, searching for answers to heal my internal wounds and calm my destructive spirit. Despite myself, God used my weaknesses, fear, critical, and stubborn nature to save my life. *"And we know that in all things God works for the good of those who love him, who have been called according to his purpose."* (Romans 8:28). *"The Lord is my light* and my salvation; whom shall, I fear? The Lord is the stronghold of my life; of whom shall I be afraid?" (Psalm 27:1).

"You, O LORD, keep my lamp burning; my God turns my darkness into light. With your help I can advance against a troop; with my God I can scale a wall. As for God, his way is perfect; The word of the LORD is flawless. He is a shield for all who take refuge in him."(Psalm 18:28-30)

"...God will grant them repentance leading them to a knowledge of the truth" (2 Timothy 2:25). Throughout this awakening, I struggled. I liked the idea of change, but hated the process. At times, I did not feel God working in my life until He revealed that patience was a companion to wisdom and how my inflictions intensified my faith. And as the cemented places around my heart were being chipped away, I recognized that my fall did not happen overnight, nor would my healing. It was not until I stopped trying to process my past with worldly skills that I began to embrace what God offered me. I eventually learned that I could not do anything alone, but God granted me repentance by His grace. A significant step in my changing process was not trusting my thinking because it kept me in a self-pity and depressive mode. Instead, I had to learn to accept and use my weaknesses to glorify God. I also had to trust, at my core, the information being revealed to me through Scripture so that it could nourish my soul. By opening the eyes of my heart, I allowed God in for healing.

Eventually, I could receive God's Word as I gradually died to my old ways of thinking and doing things. I was being reborn internally, taking on a new identity in Christ. I am not claiming to be perfect. On this side of heaven, I will forever be a work in progress. But by God's grace, I am allowed to be in His presence because of the shedding of Jesus' blood. My past has been the bridge to this revelation in my life, which has enabled me to correctly label my past situations for what they are—simply memories, life experiences, and lessons. I can now go to the foot of the cross to die to my sinful nature with the power of the Holy Spirit living in me as I put to death my sinful mindset. Oddly, my memories and sinful nature still hover around me. Any misstep that takes my eyes off God sends me traveling back into that black hole of my old dysfunctional core beliefs. Because the world seems so real, it is a constant battle to keep my faith at a level wherein I can continue to believe internally and intimately in God's promises and the life He is offering. *"I pray that out of his glorious riches he may strengthen you with power through his Spirit in your inner being, so that Christ may dwell in your hearts through faith..."* (Ephesians 3:16-17).

God's offer of life is an open invitation that comes to you through your immaterial heart and soul. Life is what God is offering you; however, it must be awakened and internally transformed toward His likeness. This life will change your soul, which includes your will, intellect, mind, emotions, and all the immaterial things that make you unique. Your trinity (body, soul, and spirit) was altered from conception, and now you need to reprogram your soul to The Creator. The skills you learned have enabled you to win some battles, but you are losing the greater internal war of being transformed for salvation. Your attachment to the physical world, your character, and your worldly thinking cannot get you to heaven. Let me rephrase that: you were created with a deep desire for God but reprogrammed by this fallen world to look outside yourself for what you need to please your physical body. If you are not intentional, your physical body can easily take control and lead your soul and spirit.

Presently, the world is in a state of confusion and chaos as it applies self-defeating philosophical strategies. At some point in our lives, we have all been exposed to various types of hurts and societal demands, some of which cause us to develop distorted perceptions, prejudices, selfishness, etc. Since we have little or no control over the world, we can spin into a vicious cycle. This cycle can lead us to form habits that fix us in a primitive mode of thinking. This leads us to pursue worldly trinkets that are externally worn instead of the heavenly jewels of inner truth, honesty, love, and respect. Holy skills will lead you back toward God's plan of salvation. (See diagrams—'Disheveled boy and Heavenly jewels—basketballs').

As those worldly strategies are being used to maneuver through this life, they have kept God's creation, "you," chemically off balance. Dr. Outley used an excellent analogy for this perspective: it is like using a map of Texas to reach Italy. He would say, "No matter our level of education, intelligence, upbringing, religion, or social status, using the wrong map can only direct you to the wrong places." To put it in a biblical perspective, it is using worldly concepts to find heaven and the meaning of life. But worldly thinking will not get you there. A lack of balance between body, soul, and spirit (your trinity) only drives your inner dysfunctionalities to create more instabilities and insecurities. *Changing the Way You Change* views the harmony between body, soul, and spirit as the starting point for transformation. They are undeniably separate and distinct from each other, yet they work as one whole unit that cannot be separated. *"The body is a unit, though it is made up of many parts... they form one body"* (1 Corinthians 12:12).

WORLDLY TRINKETS VS. HEAVENLY JEWELS

Causes: internal and external pain, emotional turmoil, bad attitude, and negative thinking. The "you" remains "sick" because of an inability to recognize and own up to who you really are internally or who you have become. Or have you made the mistake of thinking that people are the problem when it is a battle within you? This has led you to wear a psychological mask to hide behind and disguise your dysfunctional self and weaknesses. By not changing yourself from within, you have been falsely enchanted (delighted, charmed, entranced, bewitched, hypnotized, and captivated) with wrong drives, motives, understanding, and information.

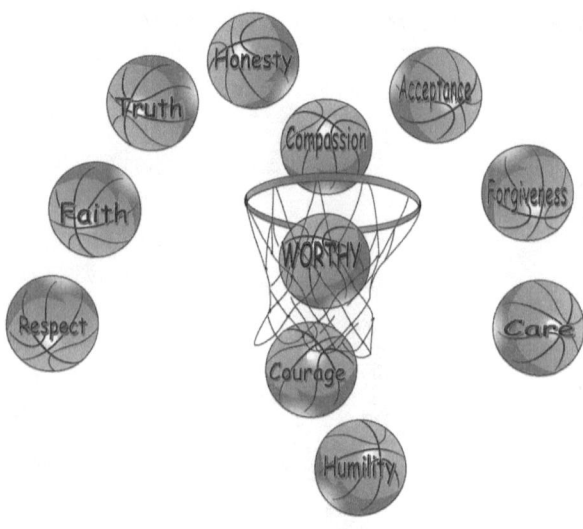

Love | Respect | Truth | Honesty | Care | Compassion
Humility | Forgiveness | Acceptance | Faith | Courage
Strength | Direction | Productivity

A balanced system will enhance your social, emotional, physical, and spiritual life. Being human comes with legitimate needs for survival. Your basic material needs are simply the things you need to keep your physical body functioning, preferably at peak level. However, your soul and spirit also have needs to keep them working optimally. You cannot take enormous energy from one area to satisfy another without getting out of balance. Many, if not most, of life's problems come from your quest to meet the basic needs of your flesh while neglecting spiritual and soulish needs. My working definition of soul includes self-knowledge, intellect, behavior, attitude, motivation, will, etc. Internal needs do not necessarily stem from a lack of something but from that core desire to grow and change. As you gave much attention to satisfying your fleshly needs, your body produced (or did not) chemicals to combat your over- or underindulgence. Excess or insufficiency in any area of your body's chemical system is not the main point. The problem lies in how you go about satisfying your needs.

Our brain is naturally wired to respond to internal and external threats with a fight-or-flight response *(see Chapter 5, 'I See You')*. Internally, at the biochemical level, humans have created an internal mess because we failed to use our caregiving instincts to provide self-support to keep us safe internally. (Side note: We have overlearned from all the negative experiences in our lives.) A healthy body starts from the inside. But sin and other worldly influences divert our path away from God. The image of God in you has been damaged, but be encouraged; it has not been destroyed or removed. Again, *Changing the Way You Change* starts with identifying and reassessing the core personal values, biases, core beliefs, and principles that drive you. This assessment will lead you to a better understanding of who you have become. Even when not acted out, your thoughts can still produce a buildup of chemicals in your body, which causes an imbalance. Nevertheless, be encouraged regardless of your age or situation: it is not too late to start changing, but it is too soon to quit.

"...keep [yourself] from being polluted by the world" (James 1:27). *"...Though outwardly we are wasting away, yet inwardly we are being renewed day by day"* (2 Corinthians 4:16). I pray you are having an internal conversation with God that will resonate deep in your soul. Remember that actual change is not about just doing things differently or improving your behavior without a heart change. Neither is it burying your feelings, nor simply hoping to be better. Through my own experiences, I continue to learn that the very heart of my Christian faith is centered on

internal growth. It is living a new life with God as my navigator to heal the pain and stitch up the emotional wounds. It means freely sharing myself with others without guilt, shame, or regret. It also means putting aside my cultural beliefs, biases, and selfishness. Actual change is getting out of my comfort zone and adjusting my soul (self-knowledge, intellect, behavior, attitude, motivation, will, etc.) to glorify God. *"Therefore, if anyone is in Christ, he is a new creation; the old has gone, the new has come!"* (2 Corinthians 5:17).

In the words of Keith Kennedy's poem "The Bottom Line,": "Nobody owes you a living. What you achieve or fail to achieve in your lifetime is related to what you do or fail to do." What you practice is what you become competent and efficient in.

WORKSTATION 1

"Consider it pure joy, my brothers, whenever you face trials of many kinds, because you know that the testing of your faith develops perseverance. Perseverance must finish its work so that you may be mature and complete, not lacking anything" (James 1:2-4). The following might help you identify possible faulty core beliefs. Some examples of inappropriately adapted core beliefs might be feelings of not being enough or accepted, unlovable, people cannot be trusted, constant self-doubt, lack of internal joy, unforgiveness, etc. If these pessimistic core beliefs are left unchecked, they allow the world to choke you spiritually, hindering you from pursuing who you were created to be.

Meditate on the questions below. These questions should be answered promptly, but with a deeper search of the heart. Take one or two at a time. Do not overthink the questions; use only the understanding you get from reading them. Fight your urge to dismiss questions for lack of knowledge, as this can be a way of not addressing the internal "you." Avoid giving padded, deflective, or vague responses; search your heart, be honest with yourself, and pray for God to open your heart so your mind can understand His truths. Treat the workstations like a diary. Remember: you will get out of the workstation what you put into it.

1. **What are you living for? And how will you recognize and fulfill its obligations?**

Your thoughts now:

_____

_____

_____

_____

Your thoughts after praying and meditating:

_____

_____

_____

_____

2. **How do you let your past experiences dictate or impact your present situation in life?**

    Your thoughts now:

    _____

    _____

    _____

    _____

    Your thoughts after praying and meditating:

    _____

    _____

    _____

    _____

3. **Are you responsible for yourself and your reactions in all situations?**

    Your thoughts now:

    _____

    _____

    _____

    _____

Your thoughts after praying and meditating:

_____

_____

_____

_____

4. What triggers your negative feelings, and how do you handle them?

Your thoughts now:

_____

_____

_____

_____

Your thoughts after praying and meditating:

_____

_____

_____

_____

5. What causes you to react to other people's outward appearances, displayed behaviors, and reactions?

Your thoughts now:

_____

_____

_____

_____

Your thoughts after praying and meditating:

_____

_____

_____

_____

6. Do you undervalue yourself when God has placed a high value on you?

Your thoughts now:

_____

_____

_____

_____

Your thoughts after praying and meditating:

_____

_____

_____

_____

7. If you believe God is telling you the truth, then why do you not behave like He is telling you the truth?

Your thoughts now:

_____

_____

_____

_____

Your thoughts after praying and meditating:

_____

_____

_____

_____

8. During your trials, what does your behavior say about what you
   believe? List your behaviors and thoughts to determine your
   thought patterns.

   Your thoughts now:

   _____

   _____

   _____

   _____

   Your thoughts after praying and meditating:

   _____

   _____

   _____

   _____

9. What are some core negative lies you believe about yourself?

   Your thoughts now:

   _____

   _____

   _____

   _____

Your thoughts after praying and meditating:

_____

_____

_____

_____

10. Do you like yourself? Why or why not?

Your thoughts now:

_____

_____

_____

_____

Your thoughts after praying and meditating:

_____

_____

_____

_____

AS YOU CONTINUE YOUR ASSESSMENT, BELOW ARE SOME AREAS THAT GOD SAYS ARE IMPORTANT:

Your secret thoughts and actions: *"For whatever is hidden is meant to be disclosed, and whatever is concealed is meant to be brought out into the open"* (Mark 4:22).

Your character (including your personality, temperament, ego, behavior, morals, etc.) defines you. *"But because of your stubbornness and your unrepentant heart, you are storing up wrath against yourself..."* (Romans 2:5). *"...but be transformed by the renewing of your mind..."* (Romans 12:2).

Your words and tone demonstrate the nature of your soul and are not overlooked by God: *"But I tell you that men will have to give account on the day of judgment for every careless word they have spoken. For by your words you will be acquitted, and by your words you will be condemned"* (Matthew 12:36-37).

Your deeds are activated by your faith and thoughts, which display your inward nature: *"All a man's ways seem innocent to him, but motives are weighed by the Lord"* (Proverbs 16:2).

Your attitude is demonstrated by your mindset, way of thinking, and posture toward your fellow man: *"But I tell you that anyone who is angry with his brother will be subject to judgment... but anyone who says, 'You fool!' will be in danger of the fire of hell"* (Matthew 5:22).

Your motives indicate your objectives and intentions: *"...He will bring to light what is hidden in darkness and will expose the motives of men's heart"* (1 Corinthians 4:5). *"To man belong the plans of the heart, but from the Lord comes the proper reply of the tongue. All a man's ways seem innocent to him, but motives are weighed by the Lord"* (Proverbs 16:1-2).

Your lack of love is proof of your need for a Christ-like Spirit. *"Dear friends, let us love one another, for love comes from God. Everyone who loves has been born of God and knows God. Whoever does not love does not know God, because God is love"* (1 John 4:7-8). *"But the fruit of the Spirit is love, joy, peace, patience, kindness, goodness, faithfulness, gentleness, and self-control"* (Galatians 5:22-23). *"Love is patient, love is kind. It does not envy, it does not boast, it is not proud. It is not rude, it is not self-seeking, it is not easily angered, it keeps no record of wrongs. Love does not delight in evil but rejoices with the truth. It always protects, always trusts, always hopes, always perseveres"* (1 Corinthians 13:4-7).

Your service should reflect your loving heart and obedience toward God and not toward man. *"And this is love: that we walk in obedience to his commands..."* (2 John 1:6). *"[If a man builds on this foundation...their work will be shown for what it is, because the Day will bring it to light. It will be revealed with fire, and the fire will test the quality of each man's work. If what has been built survives, the builder will receive a reward."* 1 Corinthians 3:12-14).

Your unforgiveness will hinder your growth as a Christian. Your forgiveness should not be contingent on whether your fellow man desires it or if they reciprocate forgiveness or not—it is about your obedience to God. *"For if you forgive men when they sin against you, your heavenly Father will also forgive you. But if you do not forgive men their sins, your Father will not forgive your sins"* (Matthew 6:14-15).

2

THE CREATED YOU

Knowing how you were created and who you are from within

"*When God created man, he made him in the likeness of God*" (Genesis 5:1). I believe creation is the catalyst for understanding how God uniquely designed you. Creation will let you know who you are, why you are here, and perhaps how far you have deviated from God's plan. It can also give you insight into the inner workings of your trinity (body, soul, and spirit), not only for self-discovery but to reflect the Creator's traits in even greater ways. Creation tells you how your body was designed to respond and what you must do to preserve a healthy balance. There is a lot that we will never know, but what is essential is to act on what we do know. And we know that one of the main focuses of the Bible is God's plan of salvation and our need to become more like Christ. To make changes, we must identify and acknowledge our problems and the need to transform our souls using God's principles. So, be mindful of God's house rules to govern His temple to move you toward His plan for salvation. Throughout this book, I will use the term salvation not only in the context of one's initial spiritual conversion but also in the sense of continuous, ongoing growth.

You were created to be purpose-driven. And since the beginning of creation, one's biggest struggle yet greatest passion has been discovering the purpose of his or her life. Each generation has deliberated over questions dealing with its existence. Who am I? Why was I made this way? Why is my life so hard? What does the future hold? Why is there so much pain in this world? Why do people hate each other? Why do I dislike myself? What is my purpose? Your dissatisfaction with understanding your life's purpose has made it difficult to know how and why God uniquely engineered you the way He did. Because you have lived life externally, you have been weighed down and cluttered with maladapted, learned behaviors. When you only look at where you are physically, you overlook understanding where you should be spiritually. *"So we fix our eyes not on what is seen, but on what is unseen. For what is seen is temporary, but what is unseen is eternal"* (2 Corinthians 4:18).

Therefore, you must appreciate how your trinity was designed to work together in unison before anything else matters in this world. Following your fleshly body's desires for prolonged periods damages your trinity. *Changing the Way You Change* assists you in bridging the human-made gaps between your trinity, not only to reveal your temple but to clean it continuously. *"Do you not know that your body is a temple of the Holy Spirit..."* (1 Corinthians 6:19). Learning, understanding, and accepting creation requires diligence to apply God's teachings. *Changing the Way You Change* will assist with internal selfish desires and ungodly habits as you learn how to repent from inner sins. Repentance is a relational connection to Christ. *"What comes out of a man is what makes him 'unclean.' For from within, out of men's hearts, come evil thoughts..."* (Mark 7:20-22). A true soul transformation will not occur until your spirit leads your soul and body. First, you must let God's words speak to you through reading, praying, meditating, gaining self-discipline, obeying, and then waiting on Him. By doing this, your faith will stimulate your heart. You will be able to joyfully release whatever you are holding onto when you give it to God, as your decisions turn into action. As we release those strongholds, we must also embrace the art of self-control so we will not get diverted. Therefore, do not get bogged down by various distractions, but try to understand the spirit of the scriptures. *"...May your whole spirit, soul and body be kept blameless..."* (1 Thessalonians 5:23).

Two things to spark your thinking: First, creation confirms you are a living being made in His image (Genesis 1:26-27). Although the word "trinity" does not appear in the Bible, God created and fashioned us from three aspects of himself: the Father, the Son, and the Holy Spirit, which we consider the trinity. Your trinity—body, soul, and spirit—are separate parts, but together, they make up the essence of "you." It is essential to learn to feed them separately as you discover the significance of each to meet their needs as a whole: 'you' *"...offer your bodies as living sacrifices... be transformed by the renewing of your mind..."* (Romans 12:1-2).

Secondly, the spirit of our world today is a never-ending stream of busyness and activity that encroaches on our time. Much of it is justified and somewhat necessary. Yet, it can create an unhealthy imbalance in your body's chemistry, bringing many mental and physical conditions like high blood pressure, stress, anxiety, unrest, anger, irritation, mental fog, etc. Your body and brain were not created to live in this chaotic, fast pace of constant overstimulation. You must understand that Satan wants to use our crazy schedules to stop God's seed from maturing within us. The key is not to become overwhelmed and preoccupied with worldly things. *"We are free to do all things, but there are things which are not wise to do. We are free to do all things, but not all things are for the common good"* (1 Corinthians 10:23 BBE). *"Everything is permissible"—but not everything is beneficial. Everything is permissible—but not everything is constructive."* (1 Corinthians 10:23).

While multitasking can be a necessary part of our modern world, when overtasked, you are an easy target to be triggered by Satan. You rush through life and have no downtime to reflect or meditate on God's Word or His miracles. My point! Do you take phone calls or look at your phone during mealtimes? Are you on the computer while talking to another person? Do you spend more time with social media relationships than with your family? How much time are you on your phone compared to face-to-face time with the closest people in your life? How much time do you spend in the Bible compared to social media? How much downtime do you have in a day for reflection and meditation? How much time do you spend or have for self-improvement? How much time do you spend sending texts or emails compared to knee-mails? Do you see the enemy, the thief of your time? Please understand that I am not advocating that you give up your 21st-century lifestyle or its technology; I only want you to be aware that your life is not necessarily better than your ancestors because of it. *"Blessed is the one who finds wisdom and get understand…"* (Proverbs 3:13-15).

Balance is the message, and change is the essence, core, and soul of life! Solitude with prayer and meditation allows what you receive from God to take root in your soul. Solitude is a necessity of the soul, which Jesus modeled for us. It will allow your spirit the time to connect with Christ.

"...He said to them, come with me by yourselves to a quiet place and get some rest" (Mark 6:31).

"But Jesus often withdrew to lonely places and prayed" (Luke 5:16). *"After he had dismissed them, he went up on a mountainside by himself to pray..."* (Matthew 14:23).

Let us take one aspect of your trinity at a time so you can grasp how they work separately yet homogeneously.

YOUR *BODY* IS THE FOUNDATION OF GOD'S CREATED TEMPLE

"The Lord God formed the man from the dust of the ground..." (Genesis 2:7). We are indeed made of clay and earth. According to science, every element of the human body can be found on the planet. Ironically, they can only tell us what the human body is made of through scientific research, but they cannot reproduce what we know to be a human using those same elements. God created you with a temperament, character traits, instincts, automatic impulses, and physical and emotional reflexes. These primitive instincts were not taught, but I argue they give His creation, 'you', a fighting chance at surviving physically for you to develop and mature the two higher parts of your trinity: soul and spirit. *"For if you live according to the sinful nature, you will die; but if by the spirit you put to death the misdeeds of the body, you will live"* (Romans 8:13).

Science also recognizes the many unique, intricate features of our human nature. Now, research is revealing that characteristics like empathy, gratitude, compassion, selflessness, fairness, trust, and cooperation are the natural order. These were the same characteristics science once thought to be imperfections and abnormalities within humanity, based on their previous theory of 'survival of the fittest.' This idea affirmed that fundamentally, we are self-seeking, egotistical, and aggressive creatures, only looking out for ourselves. I share this information to say that science is forever changing. With the advent of recent discoveries, more scientists believe they are beginning to discover the deep roots of humanity, which strongly suggests that good moral behavior carries excellent emotional and physical health benefits.

"For physical training is of some value, but godliness has value for all things, holding promise for both the present life and the life to come" (1 Timothy 4:8). Science has gone even further to identify the area of the brain that promotes emotions like trust, love, compassion, etc., and how people can be moved to practice kindness even when it seems to go against their self-interest (See research done by "The Science of Human Goodness: The Compassionate Instinct," edited by Dacher Keltner, Jason Mash, and Jeremy Adam Smith). Yet science understands very little about why we do certain things. As I alluded to earlier, I speculate that we first do things out of primitive instincts, reflexes, and an innate need to survive. We get into trouble when we do not self-control our innate desires. (See the diagram below on the hierarchy of human needs.)

HIERARCHY OF HUMAN NEEDS

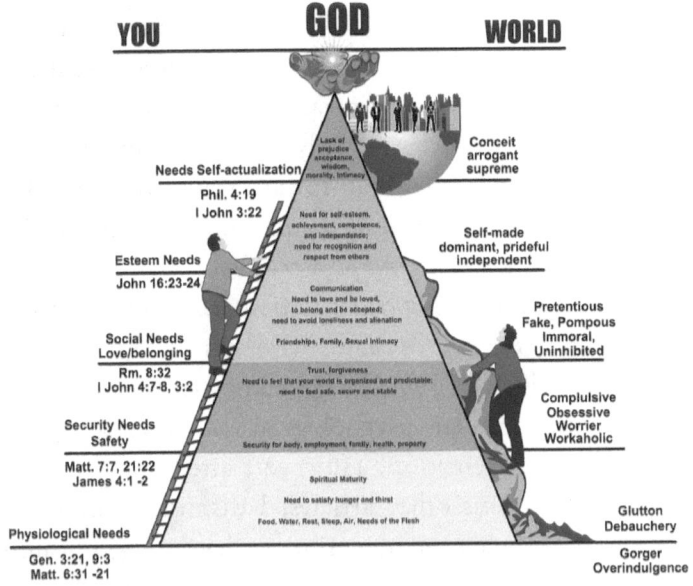

The original hierarchy of human needs was developed in 1943 by Abraham Maslow in his psychological paper "A Theory of Human Motivation." From everything I have read, it is depicted as a pyramid with the most basic and fundamental needs at the bottom. Maslow advocated that we are first motivated to fulfill basic needs before moving on to more advanced ones. At the highest level, self-actualization, you are self-aware, concerned with personal growth, less concerned with the opinion of others, and interested in fulfilling your potential. There continues to be criticism about the needs ranking based on Maslow's original research data that others have not been able to validate.

Regardless, your body has basic instinctive needs essential for survival. Without these instincts, humanity would not survive. The pecking order of needs should not be the concern, but balance should be, which is the message of *Changing the Way You Change*. There should be outward evidence of your Christian identity, but it begins with an inward change. May I say, you are not a true Christian if you are only one outwardly. A genuine Christian continues to have an inward transformation of the heart. *"A man is not a Jew if he is only one outwardly, nor is circumcision merely outward and physical. No, a man is a Jew if he is one inwardly; and circumcision is circumcision of the heart, by the Spirit not by the written code..."* (Romans 2:2829).

Changing the Way You Change acknowledges that science has uncovered excellent psychological and physical information about God's creation. However, after processing this research and various other articles, I dismissed any doubts about the Bible being the blueprint for developing a healthier me. My logic told me that science had done an excellent job of interpreting information by observing behaviors with only a trace of what it is to be human. You must have a solid creation foundation to make healthy changes to your trinity. You were made in God's image to reflect the Father, the Son, and the Holy Spirit. Metaphorically speaking, Jesus, being the Son who came in the flesh to endure life on earth, represents what your physical body can endure; the Father represents your soul that houses His character and what we are capable of achieving; and the Holy Spirit represents your Counselor and the way to commune with God where His Word is embedded. *"And I will ask the Father, and he will give you another Counselor to be with you forever—the Spirit of truth"...you know him for he lives with you and will be in you"* (John 14:1617).

32

AUTHOR'S WRITTEN PODCAST 1: In our 21st-century culture, we have expended a tremendous amount of resources and energy toward the development and perfection of our physical bodies via technology, cosmetics, diets, surgical procedures, etc. Like the Greeks during the time of Alexander the Great, we strive for the perfect body. He felt, as our culture does, that the ideal human body is an expression of one's worth, and any deformity is looked down upon. As such, our society has become obsessed with perfecting how we look. But when we divert massive energy from our trinity and expend it on bodily perfection, it leaves us out of balance. The energy needed to develop your soul and spirit is now insufficient. Be aware that any imbalance has an internal effect. For example, take the hormone oxytocin, sometimes called the love hormone; it is responsible for human behaviors associated with relationships and bonding. When released into certain brain parts, it impacts your emotional, cognitive, and social behaviors. Oxytocin allows the body to adapt to highly emotive situations (Markus MacGill, Medical News Today, 2017, reviewed by Michael Weber, MD). However, an imbalance of oxytocin can also increase deceit and envy and decrease your cooperation level.

YOUR *BODY* IS THE FOUNDATION OF GOD'S CREATED TEMPLE THAT HOUSES YOUR *SOUL*

"[the Lord God] breathed into his nostrils the breath of life; and man became a living soul" (Genesis 2:7 KJV). Your soul is the standard of life by which you live. Again, your soul is your 'self' life, your personality, nature, identity, and personage. Your brain and its chemicals fuel it. Your soul is where your mind,

will, emotions, attitude, sense of humor (or the lack thereof), and all the things that make you unique and wonderful reside. Your soul is also where most of your memory, reasoning ability, affection, thoughts, and other things in your psychological realm are located. It is the seat of passion where your feelings, fleshly appetites, and desires reside. Your body has been listening and has reacted accordingly. This is where Satan exerts most of his influence. He understands creation and how your body operates. Satan wants you to embrace the emotions that stimulate your physical body. He is counting on you not developing the inner strengths and skills to self-regulate and control your innate cravings. He knows you promoted your emotions to be the CEO in charge. So, he is relying on them, staying in charge of dealing with the plethora of false information you take in to survive this fallen world.

When you became a living soul, you were given a range of emotions with the ability to self-regulate. Any self-management you have been doing on your soul thus far has possibly been rigid and superficial since your feelings are chemically driven by your thoughts, communicating with your physical body via electrical signals. (See Chapter 3—on the mechanical brain). For the most part, any physiological arousal you experience is untrained without a self-control component. It is fixing the self with a damaged and distorted soul, thus making distortions your reality. If this is the case, you continue to grow unfulfilled with your purpose as your feelings of defeat and entitlement grow. However, we were all born with a sinful and rebellious nature. 1 Peter 2:11 warns us to abstain from fleshly lust, which wages war against our souls.

Pushing my point further, you do not acquire new emotions during your lifetime; you only learn how to control and use the ones you were created with. Raw, uncontrolled emotions do not utilize your higher faculties, which oversee your trinity to make appropriate and spiritually healthy decisions. Emotions tend to steer you to react with no spiritual component. When you act without thinking, you are concerned with satisfying yourself and become a creature of emotion. From a theoretical perspective, your physical and biological needs trump the needs of your spirit and soul. Your soul must transform to be ready for your new resurrected body for an external life that will know no sin. Where your soul spends eternity is determined by how you live now.

YOUR *BODY* IS THE FOUNDATION OF GOD'S CREATED TEMPLE THAT HOUSES YOUR *SOUL*, WHICH CARRIES HIS *SPIRIT*.

"Flesh gives birth to flesh, but the Spirit gives birth to spirit" (John 3:6). *"For it is we who...worship by the Spirit of God, who glory in Christ Jesus, and who put no confidence in the flesh"* (Philippians 3:3). The physical "you" consists of the material elements that give you an earthly consciousness. You know and experience the world through your five senses. Your soul is the psychological aspect of you with self-consciousness, emotions, free will, likes, dislikes, etc. But with your spirit, you have God-consciousness and an awareness of what relates to His Spirit, laws, and morals, with a heart to obey Him. The spirit is that part of you that can connect or refuse to connect to God. When your body is correct, you are healthy. When your soul is healthy, you are happy. But when your spirit is correct, you are righteous. You are only righteous because God lives in you. *"Don't you know that you are God's temple and that God's spirit lives in you?"* (1 Corinthians 3:16).

God is the source of your spirit and, again, the place where His seed is planted. You were designed to receive the Word via your spirit so it can mature and grow by taking root in your soul. I am highlighting that your body and soul should be directed and led by your spirit. Yet your body, with its fleshly desires, can contaminate your soul when it is in control. Your spirit is where His Spirit within you ignites your relationship with God, which makes you distinctly different from the rest of creation. You are intended to have an intimate relationship with God that reflects His love and character traits. This occurs when the planted Word of God is nourished, takes root, and is acted upon. Proof of this growth process is always evidenced by your obedience that glorifies God. Therefore, walk by the spirit, as in Galatians 3:1-5. Again, your spirit is inseparably united with your soul; however, it is not identical to the soul. The diagram below shows how your trinity is interwoven but separate (Circle of life).

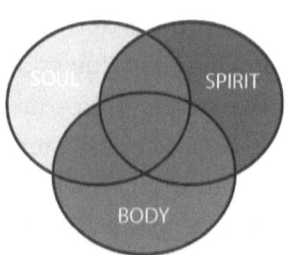

You receive the spirit of godly faith, hope, and worship through your soul. Your spirit is that inner place, the holy or holiest part of you, where God plants His seed. Luke 8:11 indicates that His Word is the same for everyone; it does not change. However, what does vary is the condition of the foundation of your soul where it lands. Growth occurs when a seed is fertilized and allowed to grow properly under the right conditions with suitable nourishment. If your soul is uncooperative, then growth will be stunted. Logically speaking, the word "seed" indicates it is not the full-grown expression of God, but it has all the ingredients it needs to become fully mature once it has been nurtured by your will to obey.

FOUR TYPES OF SOULS USING THE SEED ILLUSTRATION: The Bible mentions four kinds of soil in the Gospels of Matthew, Mark, and Luke: the path, rocky, thorny, and good soil. The seeds that are sown are good; the foundational ground of your soul that is fertilizing and nurturing it is the focus of determining its outcome. In the beginning, God gave you every seed-bearing plant on the earth as food (Genesis 1:29). This action indicates that seeds were good for harvesting food to nourish the body. A seed is a living substance with life in it; when properly planted, it grows. God's Word comes to us in seed form. Luke 8:11 and Mark 4:30-31 state that the Kingdom of God works like a seed. The seed is alive but needs to be nourished to produce a harvest. The condition of your soul will determine what the seed will do or not do in your life. Fertilization occurs when your soul, the psychological aspect of you, reacts to it, allowing it to grow internally. Again, the goal of a soulish transformation is for the spirit to direct the soul so the soul can properly handle the body. Hence, if the body behaves differently, the soul must communicate differently as God's seed influences it. When the Word of God ignites your spirit, it can deliver your soul. It is not complicated; it is just renewing your heart's desire to do God's Will.

SEEDS THAT FALL ALONG THE PATH are those seeds that do not take root. Their soul have been trampled for years, leaving them hardened. Hardness often leads to becoming inflexible (cynical, tough, unbreakable) and unreceptive (defensive, intolerant, unwilling), so the seed—God's Word—cannot and does not take root. Jesus describes this soil as not understanding the potential of the seed/word. The soul was not prepared to receive the seed; maybe they doubted God's love and intentions for them. It is hard for them to trust God as their prayers are not answered how they want. And their soul does not have enough conviction to soften the hardened places. So, they reject the seed/Word of God due to their own false beliefs, worldly perspectives, experiences, and distrust. They refuse to change until it feels right to them. They continue to want things around them to change because, in their minds, they are in the right and want fairness. Using their worldly intelligence to maneuver through life has only allowed Satan and his demons to come in and snatch the Word from them.

SEEDS PLANTED IN ROCKY SOIL are rooted in a complex, rough, unstable soul. Under these circumstances, some growth can happen, but it will be stunted, weakened, or both. Perhaps your soul receives the seed with joy, but your soul is too unnourished and parched to grow. In other words, it has no moisture or good, godly stuff to weather a challenging environment and situation. When testing and temptations come, your soul cannot withstand the pressure. The soul is not being watered or cross-fertilized by praying, reading, obeying, or seeking information from mature others. The world's temptations stunt the growth process of God's planted Word through your damaged emotions, ungodly expectations, and desires. Your worldly logic takes the place of God's truth. Consequently, you should be aware that even your good intentions can be distorted by faulty reasoning, which only takes you further from God. You have not embraced the art of discernment.

SEEDS SOWN IN THORNY SOIL are seeds planted in a soul that is overly concerned about the cares of this life. The busyness, worries, and distractions of this world have cluttered your mind and choked the life out of you. You tend to view God by how others worship Him, and you don't personally experience Him. Acts 20:24; Gal 2:20 & Romans 8:11. When too much of your energy and focus is exerted on this life, it prevents the seed/Word of God from developing. Within your soul, an environment must be conducive to nourishing the Word of God for it to mature. When your seed grows through the counseling of the Holy Spirit, it will automatically change your perspective. However, your will must be shadowed by your active faith in obedience.

SEED SOWN IN GOOD SOIL is knowing that just hearing, praying, appreciating, or even talking about God is not enough to satisfy your soul and truly transform it. You acknowledge that the seed in your soul needs to embrace God's truths tightly. You repent and change your behavior based on an inward transformation as you become a doer of the Word by cleansing yourself daily. You are willing to face the distortions of your soul and deal with its pain to find God's truth. Your character and conduct are more reflective of Christ. You are better able to differentiate between facts and truths. Your emotions are managed and regulated in a way that glorifies God. But when your emotions and logic collide with God's truth, you do not get bent out of shape or allow your emotions to guide you. You quickly listen to God's point of view and are slow to react to your thoughts and emotions. So let your actions, not your words, declare your inner transformation. True transformation is priceless to you as you allow the seed/Word of God to penetrate your distorted core beliefs and painful memories to receive the nutritional benefits of His truths. With perseverance, fruit is born in the form of character change. Your fruit will always be visible for the benefit of others.

God has always had a strategic plan to have a holy relationship with His creation—"you." With Adam and Eve, God walked in the Garden of Eden and freely communed with them, but God could no longer live with them because of sin. Later, the Tabernacle (tent of meeting) became God's earthly portable dwelling place among His people. (There are a lot of speculations and symbolisms for the Tabernacle, so this is just my takeaway.) Throughout history, God moved His earthly dwelling place and settled in Shiloh. "Shiloh" can be translated to mean "the peaceful one," thus, a place of rest. It was a safe place to commune with God for a short while, but we know it fell into the hands of the Philistines.

From there, Solomon built God a temple. John 2:11-22 shows that God's earthly temple in Jerusalem had become corrupt. When the Word became flesh (Jesus), He was His dwelling place among His people (John 1:14). Jesus cleared the temple built by Solomon and was disgusted by what they had done to God's house of prayer. Jesus' zeal purified the temple from ungodly abuse (Psalm 69:9). These temporary dwelling places were part of God's more excellent plan to reside in you and me. After being crucified on the cross, Jesus promised that God would send the Holy Spirit to live in you, God's ultimate dwelling place. Thus, God's plan of salvation assigned Him a permanent home on earth (1 Corinthians 6:19-20). While you have this earthly body, God's spirit is working to prepare you not only to be God's dwelling place but to receive that glorified body. (Philippians 3:21). Your worldly decisions altered the fundamental purpose of His created temple from glorifying God to satisfying self. Without a biblical and spiritual interpretation, your perspective was being shaped by the world. Therefore, God's temple within can also be corrupt because of worldly habits, biases, self-centeredness, etc. It would be best if you, too, cleaned your temple with the same zeal and disgust toward sin. Going to the foot of The Cross for your cleansing will purge any shame and guilt that might hinder you.

I present the following information to lay out a connection between God's temples. God gave precise, detailed instructions for the Tabernacle (Hebrews 8:5) and provided for the construction of Solomon's temple. God, in His precise, detailed, and intricate nature, also created you magnificently with all your internal complexities. God's manufactured temples had three courts: the main court or the outer court, the second court or interior areas, which included two inner courts. Metaphorically speaking, God's human temple, "you," appears to have parallels:

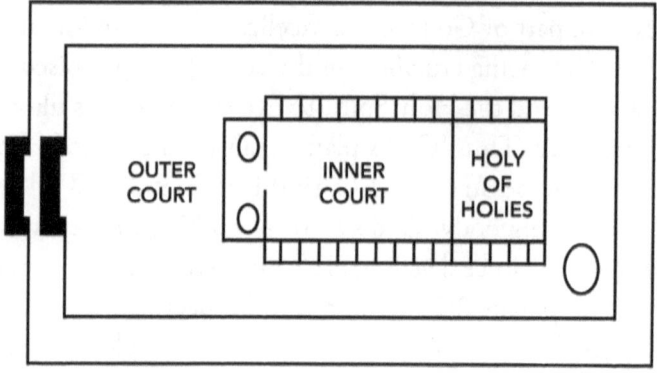

THE MAIN COURT (the outer court) was the most exterior and largest of the three courts. It was the court where Gentiles and the ritually unclean could enter. Virtually everyone had access to this court. This court was frequently visited by the sick and poor seeking help. This was where the money exchangers had crept in and were driven out by Jesus (John 2:14-17; Matthew 21:12-13). He drove out those using God's temple for the wrong reasons. Your physical body is simply the outer court of God's temple, "you." 1 Corinthians 6:19 calls your body the temple of the Holy Spirit. It, too, is the largest area of your trinity. You are not your body; however, you (your soul and His Spirit) dwell in your body. Our bodies are the first thing the outside world sees and interacts with. We, too, can use His temple for the wrong reason. It is the place, via our five senses, where virtually all the things of this fallen world can enter. It is also frequently visited by this world's corrupt and unrighteous things.

THE SECOND COURT, the interior area, was separated and entered by a gate called Beautiful from the main court (Acts 3:2). The outer portion of this second court had many chambers where special worship activities took place. Gentiles and ritually unclean Israelites were forbidden in this area of the temple. Your soul is the interior area of your temple. It is separated and entered by a beautiful opening called "you" (your fleshly appetites, desires, personality, attitude, etc.). It has many chambers where special activities take place to develop your higher faculties, mind, will, self-control, and all the things that make you uniquely you. It is the area where your offensive and defensive tactics are developed. It is designed to prohibit the unclean things of this world from entering and corrupting you.

THE THIRD COURT was divided by three steps from the second court, which had two areas attached. The first area was the House of Prayer, where the Israelites waited in reverent silence as the priests offered their sacrifices to God. The second area of the third court had twelve steps up and was the innermost part of the temple called the Holy of Holies. This was the most sacred place where the ark of the covenant resided and where God communed with the High Priest. Your spirit is the third court and was created as a Spirit-filled temple for an intimate relationship with God. This is where you should pray as you wait in reverent silence to hear from and commune with God. Deeper inside of you is your personal Holy of Holies, the most sacred place where God's word is planted to lead your trinity toward God. It is where the ark of the covenant/His holy seed resides. God's constructed temples were precious and sacred to Him, and to an even greater degree, so is His created temple—you—made in His image. God gave you a part of Himself when He breathed the breath of life into you, but you must exercise your faith to ignite the Holy Spirit sent to dwell in you. I believe this is God's way of setting apart His people by separating those who are obedient to Him from those who live by their worldly desires. And just like His fabricated temples, you should be a house of worship being cleansed daily to welcome Him. *"But the Counselor, the Holy Spirit, whom the Father will send in my name, will teach you all things"* (John 14:26 & 16:7). To expound further, I believe when you pray from your spirit, it means you continually walk by His Spirit as you patiently wait for Him to provide spiritual nourishment.

AN AHA MOMENT: When God gave Moses the designs for the Tabernacle, He was even detailed with the smallest of items. The ark of the covenant was placed in the smallest room, away from others. This room was in the center, toward the back of the temple, the Most Holy Place where God communed with man without interference from the outside world. Your spirit is housed in the smallest part of your trinity and is not visually seen by others, but it has the power of the Holy Spirit to direct the other two larger areas of your trinity. I encourage you to take some time to meditate and come to your own conviction. *"Therefore, brothers and sisters, since we have confidence to enter the Most Holy Place by the blood of Jesus, by a new and living way opened for us through the curtain, that is, his body, and since we have a great priest over the house of God, let us draw near to*

God..." (Hebrews 10:19-22). *"For the word of God is living and active it judges the thoughts and attitudes of the heart"* (Hebrews 4:12). As mentioned earlier, God created man with directives and laws to govern His creation. If you genuinely believe God is a God of order at your core level, you probably also believe He created your trinity with legitimate needs. But if the needs in any area of your trinity go unmet, it will affect the other two areas. So, having needs is not ungodly. However, how you meet those needs can be harmful to you. The way you meet these needs must glorify and honor God. Thus, it is critical not to overlook your trinity's needs in the world's hurriedness. His words are the road map and blueprint to achieve harmony within your trinity. You must follow His path without changing the intended direction to please yourself.

I understand and acknowledge that you have undergone many environmental alterations since conception. So, I assert that your God-given chemistry interacted with your mother's altered chemistry at conception. A foundation was then laid for your worldly character. Through this process, you learn behaviors for survival and how to satisfy your flesh and worldly desires. This alteration, I contend, began the development of your personality with its philosophies, biases, etc., that helped solidify your core beliefs. This, in turn, leads to the formation of a psychological mask. Masking protects you from becoming overwhelmed by events and emotions that might otherwise cause extreme psychological pain, as it satisfies your need to feel competent and safe in life. Psychological masking is strongly influenced by environmental and social factors such as rejection and various kinds of mental abuse, and it is different from blocking feelings as a survival mechanism. This is done chiefly unconsciously as a defense mechanism, so most individuals do not even know they are wearing a mask; they consider it part of who they are. I would argue that this is how your God-given natural personality changed to conform to social norms and pressures.

I want to reemphasize that the soul is where regeneration and transformation occur, allowing God's Spirit to create harmony within your trinity. When the Word of God is free to do its work within you, you are growing, maturing, and transforming. In comparison, your physical needs include but are not limited to rest, nutrition, clean water, adequate shelter, and exercise. The body will grow weak and die with too little or too much. Spiritually, you must commune with your Creator through reading, meditating, worshiping, praying, and obeying His Word. This will provide order and meaning to your life; otherwise, God's Spirit within you will grow weak and die. The needs of the soul are frequently elusive and need to be clarified. Therefore, they tend to go unmet or met in a worldly manner. The needs of your soul include but are not limited to: a) our need for socialization with other humans; b) the ability to exercise control and willpower; c) deep personal relationships that include intimate love and affection; d) acceptance and worthiness; e) obeying God's Word, etc. Without these, your soul will be crushed and weakened, and it, too, will die. (Although our souls do not literally die, they will decide where they spend eternity.) Any imbalance will trigger the overproduction or underproduction of certain chemicals in your physical body. This led to many conditions and situations that enhanced the development of your psychological mask.

AUTHOR'S WRITTEN PODCAST EPISODE 2: By various degrees, we can all agree we have needs. So, let us take our fundamental need for love. Was the love you received as an infant enough for you to develop suitable attachments and detachments in relationships to become a secure adult? Be mindful that, as a child, your subconscious definition of love was based on things that pleased you. But the Bible states, *"Love is patient, love is kind. It does not envy, it does not boast, it is not proud. It is not rude, it is not self-seeking, it is not easily angered, it keeps no record of wrongs. Love does not delight in evil but rejoices with the truth. It always protects, always trusts, always hopes, always perseveres"* (1 Corinthians 13:4-7). This sounds nothing like the feel-good, gooey type of love that pleases you with butterflies in your stomach or instant gratification. The lustful yet pleasurable kind of love secretes hormones like oxytocin, estrogen, progesterone, dopamine, and vasopressin, which are not bad in and of themselves; however, too much can be harmful, especially if it is overpowering your body over prolonged periods. Instead, if you held God's definition of love, your entire system would promote balance, be at peace, and be more capable of handling what life throws at you. God's love is genuinely concerned about the welfare of others, which will provide harmony in your body's chemistry.

The field of psychology defines personality as the sum of an individual's physical, mental, emotional, and social characteristics. I counter that personality is the organized, primitive, and self-induced patterns of behavioral characteristics of an individual based on body chemistry. Thus, my working definition of personality includes a combination of factors that form an individual's unique nature. Emotional qualities, chemical mixtures, and ways of behaving make you unique. Although most of us use temperament interchangeably with personality, we know that your temperament is nothing more than your inborn behavior patterns that get blindsided to satisfy your human desires. Science has indicated that a newborn child is not born internally blank. He or she is born with unique characteristics, emotions, and reflexes referred to as temperament. Therefore, I recognize that as a child, you had little or no control over the development and mixture of the chemistry your body created. Your interactions with your environment were driving your thinking process and emotions. Your body converted unpleasant feelings into unchecked attitudes, negative thoughts, dysfunctional social habits, and other behaviors that allowed you to live and seek physical and emotional pleasure. Your behavior and feelings were provoked into subtle, unproductive, and ungodly ways of meeting your bona fide needs. All of this happened on a subconscious level.

According to Dr. Richard G. Arno and the National Christian Counselors Association (NCCA), temperament is defined as that inborn, but not genetic, part of you that determines how you react to people, places, and things and how your environment reacts to you. For instance, your temperament determines how much love and affection you need and how much you give. Needing a little or an excessive amount is not right or wrong. Once more, it is how you go about meeting those needs. Unmet needs become your weakness, as does overindulgence. Understanding your temperament will help you appreciate the inner workings of your soul. You will accept that it is okay to have needs and hopefully identify them and learn more godly ways of meeting them. See the diagram below.

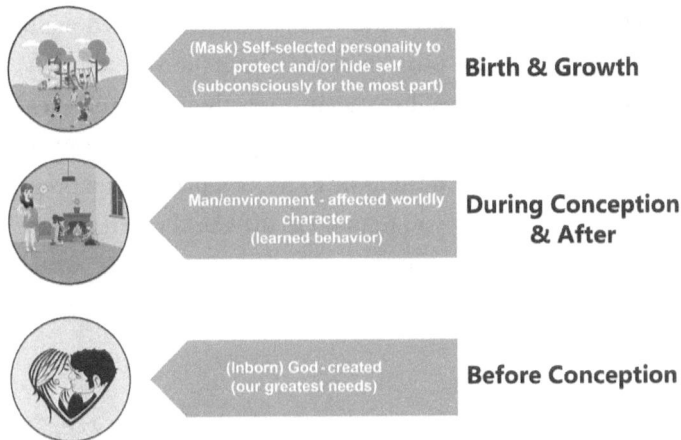

INBORN—The God-created 'you.' God created everything you need internally to be a survivor. God also created you with bona fide needs, weaknesses, and strengths. You were created with the ability and desire to commune with Him. He created your body's chemistry and temperaments, all within a complex system. As a fetus in the womb, you interacted with the world through your mother's altered chemicals, which distorted God's traits for you.

HUMAN/ENVIRONMENT (may have been altered and/or affected): While interacting with the physical and emotional world, you subconsciously develop your core beliefs, which help establish your personality with the chemicals produced. This alteration hijacked your character and established your learned behavior.

SELF-SELECTED—Your personality is the self-selected mask you display to the outside world. Your body chemistry continues to be altered by your attitude, thoughts, and even the foods you eat. Your self-selected mask is your way of dealing with (or not dealing with) people, places, situations, and things. It is how you respond to the world's demands to meet your needs, protect yourself, and conceal your weaknesses, fears, etc.

AUTHOR'S WRITTEN PODCAST EPISODE 3: *"My people are destroyed for lack of knowledge..."* (Hosea 4:6). *"From him the whole body, joined and held together by every supporting ligament, grows and builds itself up in love, as each part does its work"* (Ephesians 4:16). As mentioned, several times, you were not created to glorify yourself or feed your fleshly desires, but to glorify God. By understanding God's designed relationship between your soul, body, and spirit, you can better understand "you." Prayerfully, you have gotten some insight into how you subconsciously created an imbalance in your body's chemistry. This enlightenment should bring a new perspective on how you can change from the inside out. Strengthening your physical body happens when you get a good balance of exercise, rest, and nutrition. Strengthening your soul occurs when you implement self-control, obedience, etc. But strengthening your spirit occurs when it takes control and aligns your trinity more with God's truths and power. These efforts will counteract your misleading core beliefs. *"You clean the outside of the cup and dish, but inside they are full of greed and self-indulgence"* (Matthew 23:25 and Luke 11:39). This process will take place over time, so He warns you not to grumble or rely on your thinking. God wants your heart to honestly seek His Will for your life. He wants you to use His power to glorify Him in all situations, even when it goes against your feelings. Getting your needs met in a godly fashion is the essence of a true soul transformation.

WORKSTATION 2

This exercise equips you to assess what might be causing a breakdown of your trinity. Remember, even a single thought will elicit a chain reaction of chemicals that can affect your behavior and physical body. And these chemicals do not interpret information as false or true, accurate or unreal. So, to reduce a vicious inner cycle of turmoil for your body to respond to, you must comprehend what you have been doing inaccurately. This will also challenge your thinking to avoid generating shame and guilt.

To help illuminate your busyness, answer this question: "To what degree do you believe you are a spiritual being?" Now read the following scripture: *"Come to me, all you who are weary and burdened, and I will give you rest. Take my yoke upon you and learn from me, for I am gentle and humble in heart, and you will find rest for your souls. For my yoke is easy and my burden is light"* (Matthew 11:28-30).

Your thoughts now:

_____

_____

_____

_____

Now, find a quiet place to meditate and listen to the spirit. Then, write down what causes you to be exhausted physically, spiritually, and emotionally.

Your thoughts after praying and meditating:

_____

_____

_____

_____

Keep an ongoing list. Below are a few typical causes to consider, pray, and meditate on:

1. Physical exhaustion can occur when you neglect your body's warning signs and push it to its extreme. It can also happen when your body is not nourished with a healthy diet, rest, or proper exercise. What signs are you not paying attention to or neglecting?

2. Mental exhaustion occurs when you deplete your energy reserves. For example, when you are overwhelmed with life and all its responsibilities, you become emotionally stressed. Your body will use a lot of energy to battle that stress, thus depleting your energy source and leaving less energy for other areas. When your body overproduces chemicals over time, it can harm your body and mental health.

3. Spiritual exhaustion can occur when you expend a lot of energy doing the right things religiously but find no continual peace in your soul or joy in your life. Over time, your thinking can become increasingly negative while God seems further away. This can lead to spiritual draining, doubt, frustration, and second-guessing God's intentions.

4. Emotional exhaustion can occur when you try to abide by all the rules, but internally, you have nothing to withstand your environmental stressors. This can manifest in the low tolerance of others, inattentiveness, lack of motivation, suspicion of others, and physical fatigue. You can overcompensate for this with personal fears, tactless behaviors, and intentional or unintentional deceptions. It is essential

to keep in mind that you are the only constant variable in all situations. Emotional depletion can also result from excessive personal demands in the present or from dealing with residual wounds from your past.

The latter part of Matthew 11:30 deals with God's yoke. We all know that Jesus was born in the household of a carpenter, and numerous biblical scholars have stated that one of the primary jobs of a carpenter was constructing yokes for farming animals. The yoke is a wooden harness (collar) used to distribute the load between two working animals equally. These yokes were specific and perfectly fitted to the individual animal because each animal was unique. Accordingly, this passage metaphorically stipulates that God's yoke is specifically and perfectly fitted explicitly for you. The word "easy" in this passage has led many of us to the mistaken idea that His yoke requires little or no effort or sacrifice on our part. However, according to Strong's Concordance, some better translations would be: *"For my yoke is suitable, useful, proper, well resourced, well fitted and beneficial and not easy in the sense of little or no efforts or sacrifice."* I offer this translation: *"For my yoke is beneficial and useful and my burden is simple."* So, exercising your faith in Jesus (keeping His yoke on) causes your body's chemicals to be more balanced.

3

UNDERSTANDING YOU

The mechanical brain and its chemistry

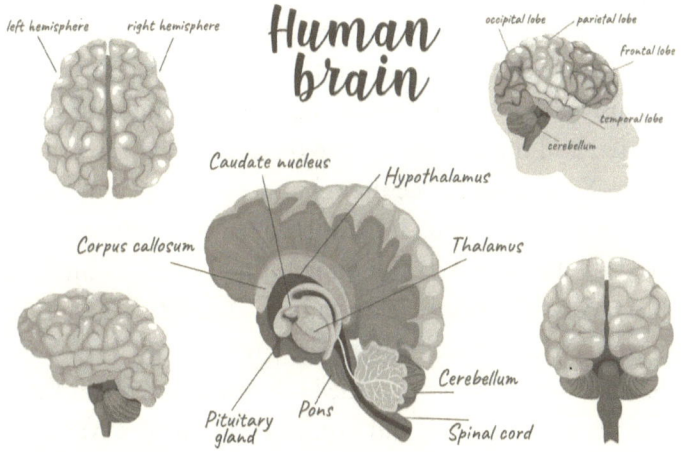

left hemisphere   right hemisphere

Human brain

occipital lobe   parietal lobe
frontal lobe
temporal lobe
cerebellum

Caudate nucleus   Hypothalamus

Corpus callosum   Thalamus

Cerebellum

Pituitary gland   Pons   Spinal cord

The Bible speaks of eternal, unchanging truths, while, as noted earlier, man's scientific discoveries constantly change. (Hebrews 13:8-9), (Psalm 33:11), (Numbers 23:19). God's creation at its most basic level is chemically driven, so it is valuable to be familiar with the basic functions of the body He created. Once you understand what God created, you will be better equipped to counteract the world's influences and make changes that will more readily align you with God's purpose and plan. As neuroscience rapidly evolves, we understand more about how our brain interacts with our environment and how our bodies are ever-changing. As newer research is being released, the information presented will be a simplified overview of how your extraordinarily complex brain and its chemicals work.

The average human brain weighs approximately three pounds and has about 86 billion nerve cells (neurons) and many more glial cells, which support and protect the neurons. The average human body contains approximately 37.2 trillion cells. Although your brain is a small part of your entire body, it is your most powerful and complex organ. It is considered the central computer that controls all the body's functions. The human brain is equipped to examine all the messages it receives, both consciously and subconsciously, as it produces thoughts, creates memories, and then plans what to do next, all within the blink of an eye. Your brain can be thought of as a sponge that soaks up every new thing to which it is exposed. At one point, scientists believed the brain had its full quota of nerve cells at birth. (see the New York Times article on January 4, 2000, "A Decade of Discovery Yields a Shock About the Brain").

Science now believes that the body-mind interaction stimulates brain cells to grow and connect in complex ways. This interaction between your developing brain's environment and early life experience creates the foundation for how you perceive the world. That foundation informs and directs your behaviors and reactions to the present day. Remember that as an infant, your interactions formed your subconscious perceptions and perspectives that developed your core foundation. The chemicals it produced established your thoughts, feelings, and memories, and vice versa.

Every thought you have is linked to a group of neurons, whether that thought is true or not, logical or illogical, good or bad. Neurologically, your body does not know the difference. Also, be advised that even distorted memories are real to your mechanical brain. Your brain only reacts to received information by producing chemicals. The secret of your emotional growth lies in what you thought, felt and how you behave which determines how you developed internally. I argue that psychological masking, mentioned in the previous chapter, produces stress hormones that keep the real, unrepentant you concealed from the public. You cannot separate what you consciously or subconsciously think from who you have become. Thus, your immaterial mind makes you who you are at your core (see Chapter 4—The Immaterial Mind).

Your brain was being redirected from what God had created, as your developing attitude about yourself, people, places, and things established your core beliefs. The under- and over-production of your brain chemicals imprinted your emotional learning. *Changing the Way You Change* defines imprinting as a form of education from conception through early development. Imprinting is nothing more than those elements of life that stick with you at the neurological level and impact you socially. This early neurological alteration is mixed with your genetics to create responses that build foundational behavior patterns. Imprint learning is rapid and often repeated throughout your lifetime.

Furthermore, experiencing intense emotional stress made the imprinting more robust and difficult to unlearn. This form of learning establishes a long-lasting effect, which can restrain you from self-regulating your emotional and behavioral responses. Let me use this extreme illustration for clarity: if, as a child, you sat by a window and gunshots came through the window multiple times, it might bring anxiety as you sit by any window as an adult, even if you were on the thirty-fifth floor with no other tall buildings around. Can you imagine certain things you have encountered and how they impacted and molded your thought patterns?

"Train a child in the way he should go, and when he is old he will not turn from it" (Proverbs 22:6). In the previous chapter, I indicated that you were first introduced to the world by the environment created in your mother's womb. Her body's chemistry helped or did not produce certain chemical mixtures and electrical wiring within her procreative body. In my opinion, this imprinting is one of the first ways your brain gets redirected away from God into a more primitive survival mode. This was early on, but it significantly impacted your development and who you have become. I am reminded of the old saying: "All I really need to know, I learned in kindergarten." This early imprinting and the innocent tools you embraced helped you maneuver and master your environment as a child. And, to a degree, they are some of the same tools you use today as an adult. However, regardless of imprinted learning, you have not stopped developing, irrespective of age. Even though your brain stops growing in size, there is continual neurological growth throughout your lifespan because your brain is incredibly complex, and new connections are constantly being made. The good news is that you can change by *Changing the Way You Change*. My logic tells me that if I embrace Jesus' teachings today, but later, my brain is affected by disease, I still win the race! This is why I love to repeat—it is never too late to start changing, but it is too early to quit.

Allow me to share this story using Alzheimer's disease: as you may know, it is a disease of the brain and the fifth leading cause of death in older Americans 65 and older. Your brain develops a plaque-like substance that causes neurons to lose connection to one another and die, thus causing brain tissue to shrink and atrophy. Simply put, it is a disease that damages nerve cells and causes Dementia. It affects your cognitive functions and causes a significant reduction in the neurotransmitter acetylcholine, which is essential for memory and learning. Symptoms include memory loss, impaired judgment, poor attention, forgetfulness, confusion, and poor concentration, along with mood and behavior changes. Multiple health issues are suspected of increasing the risk of developing Alzheimer's. Medications can only slow its progression while treating some symptoms. In other words, as of this writing, there are no known cures. (Side note: according to the AARP organization, for the first time in 2024, ways to prevent and even treat the disease are emerging.)

In 2009, my aunt was diagnosed with Alzheimer's disease. She was raised by parents who, regardless of the social injustice and hardships they encountered, always trusted in Christ, which they tried to instill in their ten children. My aunt had a quiet and gentle nature, according to her siblings.

But she strayed from her upbringing, and according to the stories she shared with me, she became "one hot tamale" in her young adulthood. Take whatever meaning you like from that term; it would probably fit her character back then.

I cannot imagine growing up as a female in her era, given the brazen bigotry and unfairness she experienced. Yet she had a strong inner desire to live the American dream the way she perceived it. I suspect she used most of her life's energy to react to those injustices while trying to reach her American dream. Time and energy were expended in managing past hurts, fears, guilt, revenge, and prejudices that created internal problems.

I also suspect she had outdated internal skills to react to her external world as an adult. Her inner maturity was inadequate to control her emotions and negative thinking. It appears she spent a lot of time getting over past hurts in order to plan how to accomplish her American dream. Yet, she had little time to prepare for a life with God. Later in her life, after much hardship, she came back to her roots and again devoted her life to Christ. She set aside all the foolishness from her youth and truly forgave those who wronged her. As a young child, I remember her preaching the Word often, even when you did not want to hear it. Auntie always had an "amen," a scripture, a prayer, and a hymn to share. In my young, unspiritual mind, she was religious and holier-than-thou, as I honestly believed she could see right through my deceitfulness.

As symptoms from Alzheimer's worsened, her short-term memory was highly affected. This distressed the family and caused some conflicts. Diminishing cognitive function led to mood swings. She was often in a state of confusion, which left her feeling anxious and uneasy. Whenever I visited her, our conversation consisted of her asking me the same questions repeatedly for an hour or so. She would mistake me for my mother and would become angrily confused about it. She often blamed family members for not caring for her properly. Her increased memory loss and confusion left our family and friends wondering about the sincerity of care each of us gave. For instance, if I had just fed her and asked if she wanted anything else to eat, she would respond that she had not eaten and did not know why I would not get her some food. When another relative came over, she would state she had not eaten in a few days and was hungry. You can imagine their reaction.

During the last few months of her life, her cognitive

functions deteriorated to the point where she became a danger to herself and was placed in a nursing facility. Her memory was almost completely gone. I suspected she felt I was a worker at the nursing home, as she could not recognize who I was most of the time. She always had pleasant things to say about others and the staff. I realized that because of her diminished short-term memory, she was unable to remember any recent wrongs done to her. It appeared she had returned to her quiet and gentle nature. I also perceived that although her cognition was not functioning well, she seemed well cared for, content, pleasant, and happy at those times. Do not get me wrong; she had difficult moments that were hard to witness.

One day, she asked why I was dressed up, and I responded that I had been to church, which opened the floodgates. She asked many questions and wanted me to read a Bible passage. She hummed her hymns and enthusiastically talked about Jesus. So, I often mentioned Jesus to divert her attention from her inability to remember. It appeared that her Christianity was the one embedded memory unaffected by Alzheimer's, even though she could not remember how to read. During this time of caring for my aunt, my oldest brother helped me to realize several important things: 1) My life is not about me and what I want from others. Acceptance is the key to changing myself for my aunt's and others' well-being. 2) You cannot force a person to remember. 3) Tones, impatience, and facial expressions triggered her agitation. 4) From her upbringing and later reconnecting with Christ, she had the spirit of Christ that did not die, regardless of other things dying inside her. Again, it is essential to grasp the fundamentals of what God created. I admit that science is gaining information about the structure and function of our brain, but again, it cannot recreate what

God created—'you.' The information science knows is only a mustard seed of the complete picture. There is so much we do not know, so why not follow the original blueprint for our lives, the Bible, to participate in God's plan? *"...I will put my laws in their hearts, and I will write them on their minds"* (Hebrews 10:16; Jeremiah 31:33). *"...he will give you another Counselor to be with you forever—the Spirit of truth."* (John 14:16-17).

Back to the brain's structure. This basic information is imperative because God created it, so stick with me. Your brain is divided into two connected hemispheres. (See diagrams on the following pages.) The two frontal lobes are the largest part of your brain and are located right behind your forehead inside the front of your skull (they are not as protected and are prone to injuries). See the chart below for the function of different brain parts.

BRAIN SECTIONS	LOCATION	FUNCTION
Frontal Lobes	Behind your forehead	Planning, organizing, problem-solving, decision-making, memory and attention. Also control behavior, emotions & impulses.
Left Frontal Lobe		Plays a large part in speech & language.
Parietal Lobe	Behind the frontal lobes	Sensation, touch, pain & integrates the sensory function from various body parts.
Temporal Lobes	On the side of the brain under the parietal lobes about eye level	Recognize and process sound, understand and govern speech & various aspects of memory.
Amygdala	Small almond shape structure in the middle of the brain	Regulate/processes emotions, control aggression, and tying emotional meaning to our memories.
Hippocampus	Seahorse-shaped structure in your temporal lobe	Helps with memory, learning & gain awareness from the environment. Connect certain feelings to newly formed memories. Alzheimer's disease affects this area.
Occipital	Lower back of the head	Visual information is processed
Cerebellum	Back of the brain connected to the spinal cord	Balance, movement and coordination

Brain Stem	Base of the brain. Composed of the midbrain, the pons and the medulla	Regulates involuntary functions necessary for survival (breathing, blood pressure, etc.). Play a role in alertness and sensation.
Hypothalamus	Above the brain stem	Responsible for body temperature, perception of hunger & thirst. Plays a role in moods and controls many hormones affecting sex drive, sleep & emotions.

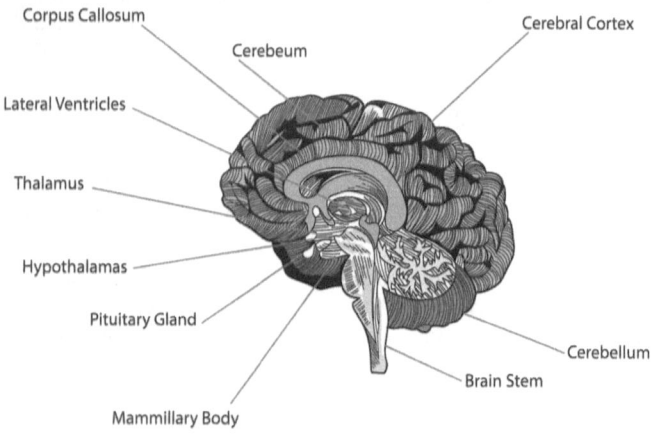

Corpus Callosum
Cerebeum
Cerebral Cortex
Lateral Ventricles
Thalamus
Hypothalamas
Pituitary Gland
Cerebellum
Brain Stem
Mammillary Body

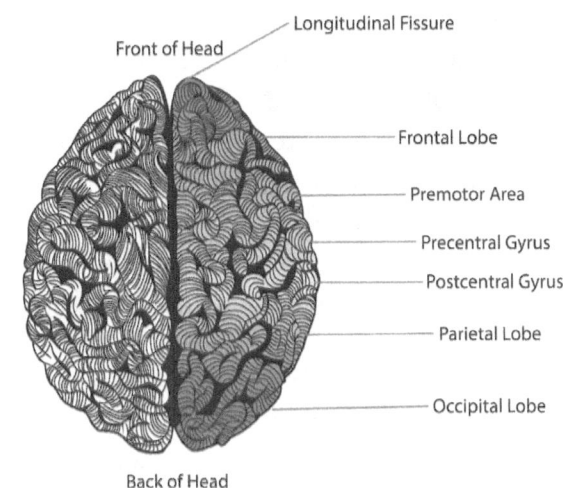

Front of Head

Longitudinal Fissure

Frontal Lobe

Premotor Area

Precentral Gyrus

Postcentral Gyrus

Parietal Lobe

Occipital Lobe

Back of Head

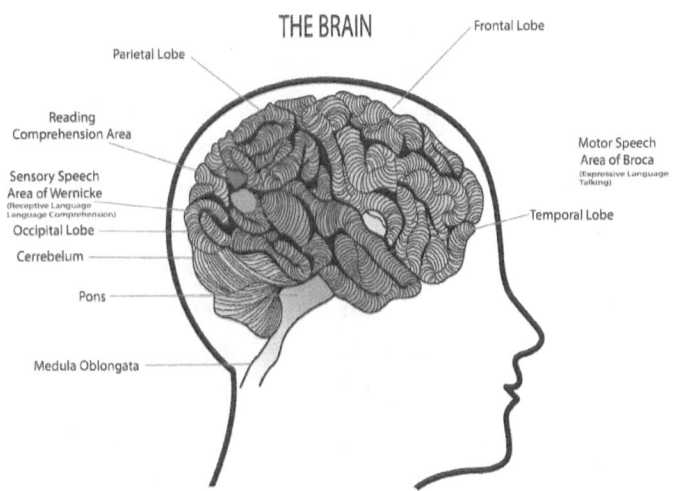

THE BRAIN

Frontal Lobe

Parietal Lobe

Reading
Comprehension Area

Motor Speech
Area of Broca
(Expressive Language
Talking)

Sensory Speech
Area of Wernicke
(Receptive Language
Language Comprehension)

Occipital Lobe

Temporal Lobe

Cerrebelum

Pons

Medula Oblongata

Most of your brain's billions of minuscule cells are called messenger cells and have a lifespan of anywhere from three days to 90 years in your lifetime. These special cells are called neurons, the building blocks of your nervous system (brain and spinal cord). Sensory and motor neurons are two types of neurons within the central nervous system. Many distinct types of specialized nerve cells conduct electrical impulses within your body. Information is transmitted through these neurons by electrochemical signaling (chemical reactions). Let us say neurons talk to each other by using electrical language. All the activity in your body originates from neurons or nerve cells and their fibers. The fibers of the nerve increase the speed of transmission of the nerve chemicals. These nerve cells carry millions of messages back and forth to and from the brain and spinal cord. Nerves do not touch one another, so the chemical messenger must jump from one nerve to the next within a microscopic space called a synapse.

For your working knowledge, a neuron has three essential parts: the soma, the dendrite, and the axon. The axon is thinner than a single strand of a spider web that carries information away from the cell. A knob at the end of the axon contains a sac of chemical substances called neurotransmitters. Neurotransmitters are the chemical messengers in the body that provide neurological information that transmits signals from nerve or muscle cells. In other words, the sac of chemical messengers called neurotransmitters converts to an electrical signal and sends data to support your body's functioning. When a neuron is stimulated, its chemical is released, causing a biological effect in your body; it must also be inactivated. When your body inactivates a chemical, it reabsorbs it to stop its action. This well-organized, complex network of neurons carries out your higher intellectual functions and constitutes your mental capacity for learning, reasoning, problem-solving, controlling emotions, desires, etc. Also, your gut has been called your second brain because it produces many of the same neurotransmitters. This is because the brain and gut are linked, and what affects one affects the other.

Note: hormones and neurotransmitters are chemicals in our bodies, but their release points are significantly different. Hormones are produced by glands and cells in many parts of the body and are secreted directly into the bloodstream. Neurotransmitters are compounds released by a nerve terminal and secreted inside your brain. Neurotransmitters are produced from amino acids via the foods you eat.

This is a bit tedious and technical, but bear with me for a little longer, as research has allowed us some insight into God's creation. All neurotransmitters are made from specific amino acids through a complex process requiring particular nutrients. These amino acids and nutrients are the only way to improve neurotransmitter levels and brain function. Every cell in your body is comprised of proteins; amino acids are the chemical substances that make up proteins. Your body uses approximately twenty amino acids and roughly 50,000 proteins for optimum health. Nine amino acids are essential for human nutrition and cannot be synthesized (reproduced) by your body; they must be supplied from the foods you eat. Newer research continues to reveal some promising findings regarding the synthesizing of neurotransmitters. Much information supports the idea of a delicate balance of nutrients needed for optimal health, but we do not know that exact balance. I want to highlight that one size does not fit all. What your body will tolerate and what your body can process with the food it takes in is individualized.

Outside of nutritional deficiencies, neurological imbalances affecting your health can also occur for many other reasons.

Some of these imbalances are caused by genetics, persistent and chronic pain, addictions, sleep deprivation, digestive imbalances, excessive use of medication, and too much stress. Chronic stress contributes to neurotransmitter imbalance and can change your brain's architecture. It affects the prefrontal cortex and hippocampus. Just know that an elevated amount of stress can kill brain cells and lead to a reduction in the size of the brain. Both physical and emotional stress cause neurons to use enormous amounts of neurotransmitters to cope, which can wear down the nervous system or even deplete the neurotransmitter supply. Although at birth, we are created with different amounts of chemicals and the ability to produce them, it can only help to clean up our diets, get off the couch to move our bodies, and implement God's words in our lives. I concur with you that there is an overabundance of information, but I am sure of three things: 1) God did not create us to leave us. 2) Balance in every realm of life is essential, and 3) no magic pills exist. But more significant than the mechanics of your brain is how you exercise your free will—what you do, eat, think, etc.

AUTHOR'S WRITTEN PODCAST EPISODE 4: SYNTHETIC DRUGS. Drugs have been known to influence and deplete the nutrients your body needs to function correctly. They affect the absorption of some nutrients from the foods you eat. Many drugs mask your symptoms while not treating the root cause. Drugs either artificially mimic the action of your body's natural chemicals or block your body from producing that chemical. What I logically deduce from all this is that if you are substituting your body's natural production of a chemical with a manufactured pill, then your body might think it does not need to produce that chemical on its own. Or, maybe the foods you are digesting interact with a drug, prohibiting your body from producing a particular chemical. Or your body might have to work twice as hard to metabolize a drug or GMO (genetically modified organism) food, etc. In either case, you have unwittingly created an imbalance. Although necessary at times, drugs can alter how your brain produces its chemicals.

I am remiss if I do not mention the American diet. It is arousing to know that the average American diet has increased from consuming about three pounds of sugar to approximately 150 pounds yearly—a 4900% increase! Sugar can be as addictive as cocaine and affect your mood and emotions. A growing body of evidence supports a relationship between depression and blood-sugar highs and lows. Although every cell in the human body uses glucose (a type of sugar) for organ function, the kind of sugar Americans intake has no nutritional benefits. Our diets do not typically provide a balance of proteins, fibers, vitamins, minerals, and antioxidants to help the body fight diseases like cancer and diabetes while also aiding in cognitive and mental function. From very early on in your life, your diet impacts the operation of your brain, something that continues throughout your life. Nutrients from a balanced diet will provide building blocks for the body and the energy supply it needs so you can function physically, mentally, and spiritually.

Just so you know, running out of energy can cause cells to die. The brain needs to be fed constantly with an adequate and constant supply of oxygen, or the neurons will die. Even a minor drop in blood sugar or oxygen can significantly reduce their functionality.

A little background knowledge of how you work biologically is extremely helpful to understand some of the complexities of God's creation, "you." And understanding a little about how neurotransmitters are produced will lead to you operating at a healthier (and godlier) level.

But for our purposes, it is enough to know your brain is electrically and chemically charged and is significantly impacted by the quality of foods you eat, what you drink, and even what you think and how you exercise your will. If your nutrition is off, it influences the delicate balance and function of neurotransmitters that transfer information throughout your body. You do not need any new science to tell you that feeding your body for optimal functioning is critical, just as providing for your soul and spirit is essential. God is loving, patient, faithful, compassionate, merciful, and so much more. It will not be easy to exhibit these qualities consistently if your body's chemistry is imbalanced. Moderation and reasonableness are keys to whatever you eat, think, and do. *"Everything is permissible—but not everything is beneficial. 'I have the right to do anything'—but not everything is constructive."* (1 Corinthians 10:23).

To demonstrate how your trinity works in harmony, consider these neurotransmitters: norepinephrine, dopamine, and serotonin. They overlap like your soul, spirit, and body (see diagram below—Circles Intertwined). Any physical or emotional pain causes your body not to produce happy brain chemicals like dopamine. If you do not regularly secrete happy hormones, a pathway in your brain is forged for you to be unhappy, unjoyful, and/or negative. Again, my point is that if one chemical is produced more or less than others, it causes an imbalance in your body. When these neurotransmitters function properly, they act like a synchronized orchestra or dance crew moving harmoniously to create something unique and beautiful. *Changing the Way You Change* is learning, through the art of discernment, how to balance and use God's instructions with the information He allows research to reveal.

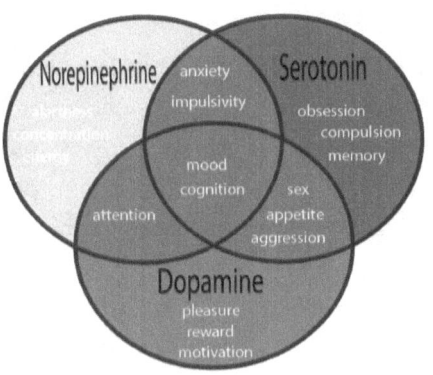

AUTHOR'S WRITTEN PODCAST EPISODE 5: RESTATING THE OBVIOUS. *"...holding on to faith and a good conscience. Some have rejected these and so have shipwrecked their faith."* (1 Timothy 1:19). To protect yourself, your false reality created both external and internal dysfunctions. In this process, your nonphysical mind emerges into the physical world through your actions and attitudes. We make choices based on what we believe, trust, and have faith in, yet what we believe and have faith in was formed from our past experiences and worldly nature. Neither your character nor your core beliefs were developed with God's truth. The fact that you think you have only promoted a type of self-protection. You only use partial and inaccurate information to maneuver through your present-day existence. Your determination and self-discipline will be of little help over the long haul. You cannot trust your thinking without measuring it to God's truth.

"I am the light" (John 8:12). Also, for all of technology's advancements and advantages, sometimes there has been too much of a trade-off in our souls. Understanding that God loves you too much to leave you in a place of defeat is essential. Now that you have a basic understanding of how your body was created to operate, perhaps you can implement changes that will help strengthen your physical body while allowing God's word to care for your spirit. *"Leave your simple ways and you will live; walk in the way of understand."* (Proverbs 9:6). *"...blessed are those who keep my ways."* (Proverbs 8:32). Training your trinity is crucial to transforming your soul for the rest of your life. (Read Ephesians 5:11-16). Your changed thoughts should allow the light of Jesus to come into your life to expose those dark and hidden areas. You will know you are changing when you willingly receive and act on Jesus' teachings.

To conclude this podcast, we know: 1) The billions of neurons that make up your brain coordinate thoughts, behaviors, and all the functions your body needs. 2) Nothing in your trinity operates in isolation; everything you think, do, and eat impacts the whole of you. 3) Neurotransmitters—your brain's chemical messengers—are made from essential amino acids, which your body does not produce independently. 4) Without a sufficient supply of amino acids for your trinity, your cells are not being optimally formed and, therefore, unable to function at their optimum level. 5) Adequate nutrition will affect the development and function of your brain's chemical messengers/neurotransmitters that transmit information to sustain your body. The right foods will determine, to a large degree, the condition of your physical body. 6) The cognitive process includes your intellect, rational thinking, thought patterns, mood, and perceptive capabilities, which are all part of your soul. 7) When you combine proper nutrition and consistent obedience to biblical guidance, your trinity will assist you in maneuvering through this world with greater ease to experience the life God is offering. 8) Your transforming nature will glorify God as His light shines in you to reach others. (Tidbit: Don't over stress on the negative or unhealthy things in your life instead concentrate on the absence of the positive and healthy things you want to include.) So, here I go again: it is not too late to start, but it is too early to quit!

WORKSTATION 3

There are a host of neurotransmitters that science is aware of, and the more familiar neurotransmitters that may pique your interest are:

ACETYLCHOLINE (ACH) controls activity in areas connected with attention, learning, and short-term memory, along with arousal associated with wakefulness, emotion, and a minor role in reward perception. It also activates motor system function and muscles, and is significant in the autonomic nervous system—a control system that unconsciously regulates bodily functions. This mechanism is the primary mechanism in control of the fight-or-flight responses, via the release of cortisol.

DOPAMINE (DA) controls aversion, cognition, working memory, sexual arousal, motor system functions, and positive reinforcement, as well as boosts mood. It can either stimulate or suppress the brain. It controls arousal levels in many parts of the brain and is vital for giving physical motivation, which is the wants and desires feature of the brain. It also controls your drive to get things done and helps with focus and depression. It is where pleasure and rewards are connected. Too much stimulation, even by synthetic drugs, can cause weaknesses.

> INTERESTING FACT: Vitamin C and copper are needed to convert dopamine into norepinephrine, which is converted into epinephrine. If any neurotransmitters' cofactors are lacking, dopamine will rise, causing the body to be off-balance.

NOREPINEPHRINE (NE) controls reward perception, negative emotional memory, anxiety, arousal, circadian rhythm, cognition, working memory, hunger, and breathing. It provides excitability and helps to make Epinephrine. This neurotransmitter can cause high anxiety levels and mood-dampening effects. It affects your attention, alertness, concentration, and energy. It induces physical and mental arousal, along with elevated mood. Low levels are associated with low energy, decreased focus ability, and sleep cycle problems.

EPINEPHRINE, also known as adrenaline, regulates heart rate, blood pressure, and blood sugar levels, increases blood flow, breaks down fats, and more. However, long-term anxiety or insomnia can cause levels to deplete.

SEROTONIN (5-HT) controls appetite, arousal, attention, wakefulness, body temperature regulation, emotion, mood, aggression, reward perception, and sensory perception. It is an inhibitory neurotransmitter, which means it does not stimulate the brain. Serotonin is a feel-good chemical that profoundly affects mood, anxiety, memory, compulsions, and obsessions. It also regulates the sleep cycle, pain control, and appropriate digestion. Elevated levels of or sensitivity to it are associated with optimism and serenity. Melatonin is made from it, which regulates and sustains your sleep.

HISTAMINE sends signals between cells. It regulates alertness, motivation, feeding behavior, energy balance, and other physiological functions in the gut. It also prevents sleep and aids with sexual response.

CHANGING THE WAY YOU CHANGE

OXYTOCIN (a bonus for your reading) acts as a hormone and a neurotransmitter. It is called the cuddle hormone or love hormone. It plays a role in social recognition, bonding, and sexual reproduction. It is thought to be involved in the formation of trust between people. Once this chemical is released, it cannot reenter the brain. So, if your oxytocin neuron receptors are blocked, there is a negative aspect to having too little. This can diminish your intimacy with others and form a disinterest in establishing intimate bonds with other people. Excessive stress, smoking, and sour foods will also inflame this hormone.

Below is your body's composition analyzed by molecule levels and the nine essential amino acids significantly impacted by the foods you eat.

BODY COMPOSITION:
55%–65% water
16% protein
13%–16% fats
6% minerals
1% carbohydrates

NINE ESSENTIAL AMINO ACIDS. Dietary research is updated often, so this is just a general snapshot. Remember, one size does not fit all. What your body will tolerate and what your body can do with the food it intakes might be different from others. It will be valuable for you to research this important topic.

1. **TRYPTOPHAN** is used to generate new proteins. It produces serotonin, and melatonin is made from serotonin (tryptophan is found in chocolate, oats, bananas, dried dates, milk, cottage cheese, meat, fish, turkey, and peanuts).

2. **METHIONINE** helps the liver process fats, and it also helps with metabolism and growth (it is found in fish, whole grains, and dairy).

3. A lack of **LYSINE** can cause vitamin B deficiency (found in green beans, lentils, soybeans, spinach, and amaranth grain).

4. **VALINE** is needed for muscle, metabolism, tissue repair, and the balance of nitrogen (found in dairy products, grains, meat, mushrooms, peanuts, and soy protein).

5. **LEUCINE** stimulates muscle protein and is thought to be the primary fuel source for tissue building when reacting to stress, infections, and trauma, and to aid in the healing process (found in cottage cheese, sesame seeds, peanuts, dry lentils, chicken, fish, almonds, oats, and rice).

6. **ISOLEUCINE** helps regulate blood sugar, regulate energy, develop muscle, and repair muscle. A lack of isoleucine causes depression, headaches, dizziness, fatigue, confusion, and irritability (found in eggs, fish, lentils, poultry, beef, seeds, soy, wheat, almonds, and dairy).

7. **THREONINE** is essential for antibody production (found in dairy, beef, poultry, eggs, beans, nuts, and seeds).

8. **PHENYLALANINE** is a precursor for hormones like adrenaline and noradrenaline. Dopamine, epinephrine, and noradrenaline are produced from phenylalanine, and a deficiency can cause lethargy, liver damage, and weakness (found in dairy, almonds, seafood, meats, cheese, lima beans, peanuts, and seeds).

9. **HISTIDINE** is an iron-rich protein that carries oxygen to every cell in your body (found in game meat, turkey, tuna, sunflower seeds, and kidney beans).

Self-reflections:

_____
_____
_____
_____
_____
_____
_____
_____
_____
_____
_____
_____

4

CAN YOU SEE ME?

The Immaterial Mind

"We destroy arguments and every lofty opinion raised against the knowledge of God and take every thought captive to obey Christ" (2 Corinthians 10:5 ESV). Technically, no part of your physical body can be identified as your immaterial mind. *Changing the Way You Change* defines your immaterial mind as those complex elements associated with your higher intellectual functioning that lie within your soul, enabling you to be aware of your environment, feelings, and perceptions. It is the cognitive executive control system for your past and present experiences. The state of consciousness is being aware of external objects and things within yourself, like thoughts, feelings, sensations, and memories. Remember that all of this is driven by your body's chemistry.

"Then he opened their minds so they could understand the Scriptures" (Luke 24:45; see also Luke 8:10). As neuroscience continues to evolve with newer findings about the brain's capacity, theoretical debates are ongoing about the levels of awareness

within the human mind. Sigmund Freud, the father of psychology, is credited with dividing human consciousness into three levels of awareness. These would be your conscious, subconscious, and unconscious minds working together to create your reality. I do not believe it is possible to quantify the percentage until we know a way to distinguish consciousness from unconscious processes. I also think that our conscious brain poses questions, while our unconscious brain uses our memory with maladaptive logic and imagination. We can dispute levels of awareness all day and still not be any closer to knowing the truth. Disputes on this topic are just differences of opinion.

Nevertheless, you can digest this information without getting jaded, as the power of the Holy Spirit ultimately transforms you. So, regardless of what I believe, some research claims that 95% of our brain's activity is beyond our conscious awareness. So, for the sake of argument, let's presume your unconscious mind accounts for approximately 30 to 45 percent of your brain's capacity. In comparison, your subconscious mind has roughly 45 to 65 percent capacity, leaving your conscious mind with only 10 to 15 percent operational capacity. If consciousness is your state of awareness, I pose two questions: 1) Out of that, approximately 10 to 15 percent capacity, how much are you using? 2) How aware are you of your internal distortions from past wounds, and how are you changing due to this awareness? The quality of information your conscious mind operates with depends on the training, conditioning, and filtering used to shape your subconscious and unconscious perspectives. Most of the information from your past encounters (with people, places, and things) is stored in your unconscious mind. Science believes your conscious mind interacts with your unconscious and subconscious mind to form opinions and deal with present issues. Your brain is recalling information from past experiences to make sense of your present, all unbeknownst to you.

Your memories are more than so-called "light switch" recollections, where you can remember what you were doing or where you were in a given situation. Your mind does not necessarily forget things; it just stores them from your conscious awareness into a different area of your brain. How easily memory is recalled depends on how it is stored, the health of your material brain, and the emotion associated with the event. If your memories were stored with false or distorted information from past experiences, more than likely, they are reacting in the present with outdated perspectives. Science tells us that no matter how detailed or clear your memories feel, they are inaccurate. ("Creating False Memories," *Scientific American*, September 1997; "False Memories," *Psychology Today*). Also, when memory is suppressed or repressed in some way, your feelings about the event may have been saved in your unconscious mind in an altered or distorted way. So, as memory is brought into consciousness, this alteration keeps you reliving the past as you navigate life. Unchecked feelings that lie deep in your subconscious are called influencing forces.

Your subconscious influencing forces were damaged and given strength by the intensity of the emotions associated with them. Now, if the filters you used in your past were cluttered with hurts, pains, fears, distortions, or any other negative information, they would continue to produce a damaging mixture of chemicals that shape your value-driven perspectives today. This is how the primitive part of your brain controls your present-day reality. Again, your unconscious mind disseminates old information, regardless of how it was stored, to your subconscious mind for your conscious mind to use today.

Let's focus on this point. The foundation for your present-day reality was obtained and saved by your unconscious and subconscious mind, regardless of whether the information was accurate, false, slanted, distorted, or somewhere in between. Also, the emotional intensity of your memory causes it to be stored with a higher probability of being recalled in similar present-day situations. So, feelings associated with those intense past experiences become attitudes and inadequate reasoning, thus prompting your body to relieve itself from stress or mental discomfort. Your past is now your present-day reality of misery, fears, and stress, which is destructively interacting with your encounters now. You are reacting to your present-day situations with thoughts and body chemicals from an outdated belief. Your conscious mind in your present-day reality should oversee your subconscious and unconscious mind by reacting to and making sense of your world.

When your present-day situation logically tells you one thing, and your emotions flare up and tell you something different, I argue you are more likely to react to those feelings via your past. This is how our beliefs, habits, opinions, and perceptions were developed and are presently being maintained. It is how triggers from past events can seem more rational than your present-day reality. It is also how mental scars from the past continue to inflame tension in your present. (Scientists continue to debate what causes this phenomenon.) So, having a negative mind will never yield a positive life. Not to sound negative, but I am only stating that letting your instincts and emotions dictate your behavior is possible without using your God-given higher intellectual abilities to direct you. When you live in the past, you take your eyes off God to do 'you.' Although I understand that you cannot necessarily change your memories, you can change the intensity of your emotional reaction to them and cultivate new memories. Through your faith, you can counter those less desirably charged memories by taking captive each unpleasant thought and making them obedient to Christ's truths and teachings.

At this time, you might be asking yourself why this vicious cycle is going on internally! *"For the flesh desires what is contrary to the Spirit, and the spirit what is contrary to the flesh. They are in conflict with each other, so that you do not do what you want"* (Galatians 5:17). For the sake of clarity: It is because the mind does not like being helpless or in a state of discomfort, so your mind will rely on old information and skills to oversee new situations. Also, our multifaceted system likes the familiar things in life to secure its fundamental need for love, stability, and safety. As such, your mind has a strategic way of interacting with your mechanical brain, turning most of your behavior into habits. This is meant to make your brain efficient so you can devote your attention to emergencies and new situations as needed. If you had to think about every action you took, your brain would be the size of Texas! Thus, for the sake of convenience, it is easier for the mind to exercise choices at the subconscious level, which draws heavily on past experiences. Again, your consciousness is recycling data from past encounters to protect 'self' and feel pleasure today. Satan wants to keep you focused on those past hurts to stimulate your body's pharmacy of harmful chemicals. And this keeps you from being able to discern your subconscious influencing factors, let alone develop mature skills to make inner changes.

HABIT—*I am your constant companion and your greatest helper or heaviest burden. I will push you onward or drag you down to failure. I am entirely at your command. Half the things you do should be turned over to me, for I can do them quickly and correctly. I am easily managed; you must merely be firm with me. Show me exactly how you want something done and after a few lessons, I will do it automatically. I am the servant of all great men; and, alas, of all failures. Those who are great, I have made great. Those who are failures, I have made failures. I am not a machine, though; I work with all a machine's precision plus a man's intelligence. You may run me for a profit or run me for ruin; it makes no difference to me. Take me, train me, be firm with me, and I will place the world at your feet. Be easy with me, and I will destroy you. WHO AM I? I AM 'HABIT.'*"—AUTHOR UNKNOWN

"*Have nothing to do with irreverent, silly myths. Rather train yourself for godliness; for...godliness is of value in every way, as it holds promise for the present life and also for the life to come*" (1 Timothy 4:7-8 ESV). As stated earlier, and I argue, your human nature and behavior are essentially habitual. Most of your reactions are repeated, over and over again, from outdated information without much thought or constructive spiritual guidance. To fully experience your reality, you must be physically, mentally, and emotionally aware of your internal and external worlds, past and present. Your internal conflicts and chemical mixtures have caused inappropriate habits that attempt to ease inner tension. You can become so comfortable with this arrangement that you consider this to be simply who you are. You can justify those feelings and habitual reactions because

God made you this way in your mind, and it feels right. This can also be why you may doubt your life and subconsciously suppress God's authority. Or perhaps you have resisted personal change as you critique the faults in others. Sometimes, great energy can be expended in a desperate attempt to protect self and secure serenity. *Change the Way You Change* by 1) giving God what you have now (your present negative thoughts, feelings, hurts, pains, etc. then, 2) identifying and acknowledging the core beliefs you hold now, and 3) seeking to understand how and why you have been acting and reacting in specific ways; now 4) develop new habits in Christ. As you welcome the Holy Spirit, ask God to flood you with His presence and enlighten your heart with understanding. The Bible states, *"as a man thinketh, so is he"* (Proverbs 23:7 KJV).

A computer analogy is relevant here to stretch my point. Like a computer, your mind is only as sound as the quality of information you program into it. You need to update your hardware and acquire new software to improve the quality of your internal character and external behavior/output. Your present reality limits your processing capability because you need internal updates via insight and change. Again, let us face it: Your true nature does not like change and can even be rejected. This may be why you are so prone to being stagnant in your spiritual growth and continue to repeat things that have proven not to work. Thus, it keeps you in your present state of doubt and misery with a false sense of serenity. Your internal doubts, shame, and fears have likely killed more of your dreams than anything else. What life has done and will do to you depends more on what is inside you! God will not force you to choose but will always allow you to choose freely.

We feel we know of God and talk about Him; however, far

CHANGING THE WAY YOU CHANGE

too many of us have only grasped the language of Christ but not the reality of Christ. We have been positioned with Jesus, but are unable to find him because of our darkness. We have been hiding in our own flesh, thus unable to experience Him at our core. To experience God, you need internal attachments to love, respect, truth, and honesty. This will help you develop the art of discernment. God did not intend for us to carry negative emotions like bitterness, doubt, hopelessness, helplessness, fear, worry, insecurity, etc. Even when you felt moments of excitement or happiness, they were short-lived and not necessarily the same as having the joy and peace of Christ dwelling within you. Counteracting a lack of joy and peace requires you to make a paradigm shift to no longer be attached physically or mentally to this world. Only a mind renewing, the inward transformation will bring about godly change. *(2 Corinthians 4:16—"...Though outwardly we are wasting away, yet inwardly we are being renewed day by day.")*. Here are some steps that might guide you toward safety and serenity to satisfy your innate need for security and love: 1) Your faith should ignite you to give God your best. 2) Your behavior will reflect your faith, which will breed genuine interactions out of love and respect. 3) Honesty will reflect your inner character, which God's truth should measure.

Identify the distortions and core lies causing discomfort as you seek to experience God's presence. This will be the internal work God wants to complete in you. Suppose peace is not experienced in a situation. In that case, you might be holding onto something in your core beliefs that is overpowering your experience of God at that moment. True transformation is experiencing God's power in all situations to His glory. Again, our human mind wants stability, so it will default to what it knows best. But God's ignited power inside of you will allow you to use your God-given gifts to better manage your behavior. God wants you to choose Him behaviorally, emotionally, and spiritually. He desires you to identify how Satan's deceitfulness is influencing you so you may gain a higher level of freedom. Be aware that your real struggle is whether you will yield to your worldly desires or surrender to the Spirit's demands. This will be your internal battlefield until you leave this earth. So, I encourage you to be a vessel God can use. None of this is about you being perfect, but about constantly taking steps toward internal changes. *"For the eyes of the Lord range throughout the earth to strengthen those whose hearts are fully committed to him"* (2 Chronicles 16:9).

Be cautious because when we get used to doing things our way, we forget to seek God's way to experience Him in the here and now. The following two cases will identify some internal pitfalls:

CASE 1. *"For though we walk in the flesh, we are not waging war according to the flesh. For the weapons of our warfare are not of the flesh but have divine power to destroy strongholds"* (2 Corinthians 10:3-5 ESV). *"Be diligent in these matters; give yourself wholly to them, so that everyone may see your progress"* (1 Timothy 4:15). In 2014, I met a young woman who presented herself as a strong, independent person who had an inborn ability to tackle any obstacle put in her path. She talked about the faults of others as though she were seeking God's approval to help them. After getting to know her, I learned that as a child, she felt abused and neglected by others. In her opinion, others did not see her as being worthy. She subconsciously adopted low self-esteem based on what she learned to believe about herself. She often talked loudly to intimidate others, challenging them to feel heard.

She felt that being aggressive and loud would prevent potential disapproval and mental abuse. She constantly attempted to prove herself and had become overwhelmed with living for this approval. She was riddled with insecurities and an internal fear of being unloved and unseen. As she developed a defensive character, unbeknownst to her, it was laced with negativity and sarcasm. She used her destructive arsenal of worldly skills to maneuver through her life, attempting to satisfy her need for love and worth.

Even her excessive service to others was a selfish ploy to feel accepted, as she used the action of serving to get others to love her. All these behaviors only depleted her body of the energy needed for the other areas of her trinity. She often said, "This is just who I am; if you love me or are a devoted friend, then you will accept and understand me. God knows my heart." She had a way of talking godly but with no real visible transformation. Her partial core beliefs appeared to be: 1) She saw herself as inferior and tried to compensate for this flaw by being overly aggressive. 2) Not wanting to appear weak. 3) Using verbal aggression as a strength to gain control and appear worthy, needed, and respected by others. 4) Needing unconditional love and acceptance that was being fulfilled in ungodly ways. 5) Mistrusting the intent of others. Any mention of change was problematic for her to hear because, in her mind, she felt she was doing what God wanted, as she concentrated instead on the faults of others. Her thought pattern kept her stagnant without any real internal growth. She held snippets of truth, but they were all externally oriented. Her encounters with others were characterized by self-preservation tactics with no in-depth insight regarding her transformation. She continues to use these skills as she maneuvers through this world.

CASE 2. *"Sow for yourselves righteousness, reap the fruit of unfailing love, and break up your unplowed ground; for it is time to seek the Lord...You have depended on your own strength"* (Hosea 10:12-13). Although substance addictions are often the easiest to recognize, addiction can take many forms. An addiction is simply a compulsive habit-forming need (physical or psychological) for a thing or activity. Psychological obsessions and compulsions can be the toughest to overcome. These take hold in our internal deceptions and insecurities. Even simple things like technology have tempted us to indulge our addictive nature. The compulsive use of social media has become a way for some to hide their true selves. We lick past wounds and pacify our innermost worldly desires, all to find relief and pleasure. Again, Satan does not want you to develop the skills to control your God-given faculties. Satan has ambushed and confused us all as we turn inward toward self-preservation.

My reality was altered when Satan used my internal pharmacy of chemicals to produce my innate addictions. My addiction was a psychological self-dependence, and like all addictions, it affected me physically and mentally. I kept an external focus for years while my past wounds and hurts went unchecked. I concentrated on things others did and did not do. I became so obsessed with fixing others and looking at all their faults that I had little time and energy for self-improvement. God had no real power in my life because I was in control. I had developed a psychological addiction to the things that fueled my thoughts from past regrets, hurts, guilt, and shame. This was one of Satan's schemes to control my will and take my eyes off Jesus. To quote William Booth, *"These are things all outside of a man if the inside remains unchanged you have wasted your labor. You must somehow graft upon man's nature a new nature, which has the element of the Divine."*

My psychological addictions can be characterized as compulsive behaviors and thinking patterns that were an attempt to reward myself despite adverse consequences. My dysfunctional thinking was in control, igniting the production of my body's chemistry like alcohol and drugs stimulate the body. My mental desire to create pleasurable feelings about myself fed my insecurities. It gave me a worldly way to reward and reinforce pleasant feelings and stimulating attachments. Over-indulging my faulty thinking caused increased adrenaline production along with other body chemicals. This created a critical-like thought pattern that fed my justifications for feeling good about myself. But my body gradually required increased adrenaline to achieve the same effect. Although I may have appeared strong and self-sufficient, my psychological addiction blinded me as it grew in my present reality. I collapsed emotionally after many years of hiding, being miserable, and doing things my way. Yet, my curious nature needed to be fed to understand how Satan's schemes controlled my mind and why I was so miserable.

Going back to my roots, I looked to Christ for answers. In my search, I was led to scriptures like: *"The acts of the flesh are obvious: sexual immorality, purity, and debauchery; idolatry and witchcraft; hatred, discord, jealousy, fits of rage, selfish ambition, dissensions, faction, and envy; drunkenness, orgies, and the like. I warn you, as I did before, that those who live like this will not inherit the kingdom of God"* (Galatians 5:19-21). *"Her nights will be dark, without a single lamp. There will be no happy voices of brides and grooms. This will happen because her merchants, who were the greatest in the world, deceived the nations with her sorceries"* (Revelation 18:23 NLT 1996). I understood the sins mentioned in these passages, but failed to know how they applied to me internally. I concentrated on the external 'me,' which distracted me from examining the internal 'me.' Eventually, my curiosity lured me to focus on words like "sorcery" and "witchcraft" in the scriptures mentioned above. I ignored such terms in the past because I connected them to medieval times and viewed them as unrelatable.

I found approximately 30 scriptures using some form of the word "sorcery" in the Bible. And different versions of the Bible using other translations. But, regardless of the translation, sorcery, magic spell, etc., it refers to evil, immoral, false, and deceptive practices that seek to bypass God's wisdom and sovereignty. I learned that sorcerers in biblical times used their drugs—or "potions" as they called them—to stimulate hallucinations as part of their pagan religious practices. None of this had any real meaning for my life in the twenty-first century. But as I looked deeper, it brought me to the following conclusion. Satan uses the magic spell of alcohol and drugs to deceive some into taking their eyes off Christ. For others, he uses the body's pharmacy produced by wounds from their past to keep them distant from God. He used my innate need to be strong and self-sufficient to lure me away from God's authority. Regardless of what you believe about spirits and other things, the worst part is that we are intoxicated and numbed by substances from outside and inside our bodies. These excessive substances weaken the body, leaving us in no shape to fight Satan's attacks. I believe it is safe to say that any addiction has the power to ruin our lives and relationships. Whether synthetic drugs or our body's own chemicals produced our addiction, it has taken our attention away from God and opened us up to spiritual attacks as these self-stimulating practices set up strongholds.

At this point, a highly damaging byproduct of our struggle has been the inability to make the teachings of Christ attractive to others. *"...so that in every way they will make the teaching about God our Savior attractive"* (Titus 2:10). The magic of any transformation will happen outside of our internal comfort zone. So, when we hide within ourselves, we are not transforming. Please note that what you learn today will have a profound impact on your tomorrow. And what you achieve or do not achieve today was determined by what you learned yesterday. So, what you do today will be more important than what you did yesterday or what you might do tomorrow, because nothing will happen unless you take the first step toward change. Rethinking how you change is about challenging your mind to be less influenced by the external things that keep God at a distance. You then can acknowledge that you are a work in progress and who you are in Christ as someone who no longer allows the past to control you. You no longer need to blame others, lick your wounds, or stew over what could have been. To the measure you sow, you shall reap. Be reminded that a single thought can change your life for good or bad. So, the challenge is to avoid excessive stress, which creates an imbalance of bodily chemicals. Also, remember that your mind's main quest has been a pursuit for survival and pleasure, but left unchecked, these will continue to contribute significantly to your imbalance. I believe better mental health is a cornerstone of living for Christ. *"...a precious cornerstone for a sure foundation; the one who trusts will never be dismayed."* (Isaiah 28:16).

Grasping the significance of your mental health as you examine your core beliefs is imperative. This book expresses that truth, honesty, faith, trust, obedience, and courage are the six essential core values needed for a productive life in this present world. Your heart's core desire should be the courage to implant honesty, shown by your growing faith as you embrace God's truths, demonstrated by your will to obey and trust in

Him. Once again, your faith grows daily by hearing, praying, obeying, and meditating on the Word of God via your spirit. It matures within your soul and ignites your heart by your will to obey. And with that heartfelt mindset of obedience, your body produces constructive and balanced chemicals. You are dying to self and transforming into God's image as your heart drives you to experience Him at that deeper level (in your holy of holies).

As stated before, *Changing the Way You Change* involves you doing things His way, even when it feels unnatural or difficult. As this transformation continues within you, you should no longer want to conform to your ungodly, old lifestyle. The book of Romans discusses Paul's deep frustrations when he realized his sinful nature refused to obey God's laws. Paul's body had been conditioned to respond to its sinful nature. Like you, Paul wanted to do what was right: *"I do not understand what I do. For what I want to do I do not do, but what I hate I do. And if I do what I do not want to do, I agree that the law is good... I know nothing good lives in me, that is, in my sinful nature. For I have the desire to do what is good, but I cannot carry it out. For what I do is not the good I want to do, but the evil I do not want to do—this I keep on doing"* (Romans 7:1519).

Your life exists between conception and death, requiring continual growth to transform into God's ripe fruit. So, like Paul, you cannot dwell on your weaknesses as the root of your problems, for this only keeps you a prisoner within yourself. Be encouraged that God continually gives you His grace to transform your inner being while on Earth. I know it can be incredibly challenging to live righteously, but remember, forgiveness (past, present and future), was purchased on the cross to pay for our sins. Reading the Bible, praying, and obeying the Holy Spirit are vital for overall health. *"But if Christ is in you, your body is dead because of sin, yet your spirit is alive because of righteousness"* (Romans 8:10). God wants from you a willing spirit of submission that changes your soul. Surrendering your will to God will require you to act on faith. If you believe God's truths, show it by obeying and behaving accordingly! Changing your mind and your actions will guide your path. You must believe that everything will be all right in the end; if it is not, then it is not the end! If God said it, that settles it, at least, to the extent that you believe it. Now, do it and live it!

AUTHOR'S WRITTEN PODCAST EPISODE 6: *"Do not conform any longer to the pattern of this world but be transformed by the renewing of your mind. Then you will be able to test and approve what God's will is—his good, pleasing and perfect will"* (Romans 12:2). Do not make life more complicated than it is. Thus far, your worldly knowledge has dominated your perceptions of God over experiencing His presence in your life. Every new experience you encounter has been perceived through the lens of earlier memories. Scratching the surface of a relationship with God has been all you felt comfortable doing because of the internal pain from your past. Let me use this 'ouch' real-life analogy. In 2010, my teenage nephew was severely burned by a gas fire and had to undergo an excruciatingly painful process to heal properly. His wounds were scraped to remove debris and lessen the potential for infection beneath the skin's surface, which could cause problems with his organs. Although extremely painful, the scraping was vital for healing to occur. This scraping process had to be repeated several times before allowing new skin to form on the outer surface. Can you see the continual need to scrape off the worldly layers infecting your trinity? Your soul's spiritual healing and transformation will not occur until this is done.

Worldly knowledge can help you superficially, but it cannot deliver true freedom. No person, not even Satan, can control your will without your permission. Satan can only tempt you with your heart's lustful desires. But know it is you who gives Satan access and permission. I need to state the obvious: Satan was defeated on the cross and has no physical power over us. We listen to his verbal thoughts in our minds while he sits back and watches our emotions take over. To be soulishly transformed, your mind needs constant spiritual renewal. A focus on proactive self-development will keep your transformation process on track. Exercising self-control and using your mind productively will also bring some success. Beyond that, applying God's Word, accepting His grace, and obeying His Word should alter you internally. This process will drive your soulish transformation, moving you toward becoming who you were created to be.

I read somewhere that once your mind stretches with new ideas, it never returns to its original dimensions. With that said, your heart must allow your mind to be strengthened and stretched as you walk closer to Christ. Be aware that for your mind to protect your trinity adequately, you must develop appropriate routines such as scheduled times for resting, exercising, good nutrition, and maintaining healthy relationships. *"I the Lord search the heart and examine the mind, to reward a man according to his conduct, according to what his deeds deserve"* (Jeremiah 17:10).

WORKSTATION 4

In the last few years, there has been an enormous interest in emotional intelligence (EQ). EQ is the ability to understand, use, and manage your emotions in positive ways. EQ helps you handle interpersonal relationships, express one's emotions, to relieve stress, perceptive, regulate emotions, etc. It connects you to your feelings, turns intentions into actions, and makes informed decisions about what matters most to you. EQ is the key to personal, professional, and spiritual success. Key Elements: empathy, self-control, self-awareness, self-regulation, motivation, and Godly social skills. I believe your EQ is more important to Christ than your IQ.

Read Proverbs 4–Wisdom is Supreme

Your thoughts now:

_____

_____

_____

_____

Your thoughts after praying and meditating:

_____

_____

_____

_____

Self-reflections:

_____

_____

_____

_____

_____

_____

_____

_____

_____

_____

_____

_____

5

I SEE YOU—THE EXPRESSIVE YOU

If you believe God's words, behave like He is telling you the truth to stop the vicious turmoil in your mind.

"Have nothing to do with godless myths...rather, train yourself..." (1 Timothy 4:7). The quality of your emotional life says much about who you have become. Like it or not, you have become emotionally oriented to this world at some level. Because sin has an uncanny way of creeping into your emotions, it can make you feel hurt, sad, doubtful, prideful, and guilty, which can be damaging. This life is not a matter of being right, especially when your thinking pattern has colored and distorted your present mental vision. Although your life may be weighted down, a significant part of *Changing the Way You Change* will be seeing the real "you" and owning up to who you have become so you can reflect Christ. Therefore, understanding your emotions will be crucial to understanding how your soul can get so far off track.

The previous chapters revealed how destructive emotions resurface from time to time in new situations to mislead you. So, remember, emotions are stimulated by your thoughts processed through your distorted subconscious and unconscious filters. Emotions are just subjective sensations perceived and created by your body's chemistry and driven by the foods we eat. They can be habitually and automatically triggered in the present. Emotions can bring you considerable pleasure or pain, with the ability to excite powerful desires as they squash God's truths. At times in your life, emotions can be your best friend or your worst enemy. They are intertwined with mood, temperament, outlook, personality, and motivation. Past distorted emotions can fuel the present situation you find yourself in. So, regardless of whether your emotions are rational, they steer you into action and become the driving force of your life. *"A cheerful heart is good medicine, but a crushed spirit dries up the bones"* (Proverbs 17:22). If your mindset is not grounded in God's truths, any gains you may make emotionally or psychologically will be short-lived. I believe most of the negative emotions you experience today contain residual pains from past events. The worries and woes of this world have left you with deep emotional scars, which have hindered you from transforming inwardly. It can be tough to realize how childhood perspectives are clouding your present-day perceptions.

As this life of yours is forever being taxed, it has taken a toll on you physically, spiritually, and emotionally. And when life's transitions are incomplete, they leave deposits of ill feelings and destructive emotions. They cause your body to produce the stress hormone cortisol, which tends to create tension and anxiety, causing general dissatisfaction with life. As God's truths get squeezed out, you may feel you can master your environment, but that is misleading at best. You may even justify yourself by saying you are waiting for God to answer! May I ask if you searched the scriptures, prayed, meditated, and waited patiently on Him as you obeyed? Did you check your faulty thinking against His truth? Did you trust what you received, or are you trying to make God's response match your feelings? Once again, I need to stress this point: 'If you believe what God is saying, then behave like you do by redirecting your will to use His power to implement internal changes.' I will put it this way: if I tell you your clothes are on fire, would you passively ignore me to take care of it later? Or would you immediately jump into action to save yourself?

Your incredibly complex brain was created to do many things, like love, fear danger, seek safety, enjoy pleasures, protect loved ones, etc. It was also created with all the chemically fueled emotions you need. Although sometimes you cannot stop your feelings from coming, you can change their intensity, duration, and direction by choosing which ones to focus on and fuel. But it is conceivable that you may feel anger is beyond your control, yet the Bible tells us otherwise. In 1 Peter 5:7, God tells us to cast all our anxiety on Him; by doing this, you can, at some level, avoid the overproduction of stress hormones in your body. Now, try to view anger as a category-four hurricane: Can you see how it can destroy everything on its path?

Now imagine the emotional suffering Jesus endured on Earth, specifically on the cross! He was not angry. His pain and suffering were not about Himself and what He was going through. He cried and suffered over your sins. The nails were not holding Jesus to the cross; it was His love for you. Although His physical pain produced some cortisol, His love for you reduced it. So, knowing your emotions are chemically driven benefits you to take control of your thoughts by redirecting them and not feeding into their negativity. When you capture your conscious thoughts, it lessens your body's production of harmful chemicals. When you implement His truths, you can find ways to control your emotions.

Stress is mentioned several times, so let me shed light on what it is and what it does to and for your body. Cortisol is the stress hormone necessary to help your body maintain balance and stability. It is needed to help you wake up in the morning. It meets your body's demands by regulating your energy needs. Cortisol is necessary to help you cope with perceived or real danger (fight-or-flight response). Stress can be physically, emotionally, mentally, or spiritually induced, starting with a single negative thought. When you are in any stressful situation, your body produces an abundance of cortisol to combat its sense of danger. Once cortisol is produced for prolonged periods and not eliminated, other stressors develop and damage your body. In other words, too much cortisol lowers the functionality of your body. It can lead to a breakdown of body tissues, hormonal functions, and impaired digestion. It can also weaken your immune system and cause insomnia, weight gain, high blood pressure, depression, fatigue, heart disease, excessive blood sugar, elevated cholesterol, and even the breakdown of muscle tissues. Also, elevated cortisol levels can cause calcium depletion, leading to bone density issues. When cells are overworked, they become resistant by creating a condition known as adrenal exhaustion, also known as chronic fatigue syndrome. The bottom line is that the overproduction of cortisol eats away at your body and affects your soul, which bleeds into your spirit.

Our modern way of living has put us at an even greater risk for the chronic overproduction of cortisol. Research has revealed that staying up past midnight causes increased production of cortisol. Why? Because at night, your cortisol and adrenaline levels are supposed to drop, allowing you to sleep as your body starts producing melatonin, a chemical that helps sustain sleep. Constant stress causes your brain to be hypervigilant about negative information. I speculate that most of our overproduction of cortisol results from residual pain left over from old messes, which becomes a fertile breeding ground for new messes. I also speculate that most of your stress is from mental and emotional origins rather than stress produced by physical threats in your environment. During more primitive times, cortisol was physically sweated out of the body through hard work and other strenuous physical activity. But your sedentary lifestyle, high sugar intake, and mental overload minimize cortisol reabsorption. Remember: when your body releases a chemical, it must inactivate it by reabsorbing it to stop its action.

So, I maintain that as a Christian, your spiritual warfare has been fought on the battlefield of your mind. Ungodly thinking eventually turns into sinful desires that leave you an emotional wreck. When you are worn down, you are physically, emotionally, and spiritually vulnerable, thus unable to experience God's joy and peace. As such, when Satan sends his demons, a lack of internal well-being can cause you to give in to your sinful, primitive nature. For fun, let us give Satan's demons names so you can recognize and acknowledge some of them for what they represent. They are Mr. Doubt, Ms. Procrastination, Mrs. Complacency, Ms. Deception, Mrs. Spite, Mr. Lust, Mr. Impatience, Ms. Deceit, Mr. Dislike, Ms. Entitlement, Mr. Insecure, Ms. Arrogance, Mrs. Conceit, Mr. Self-importance, etc. These demons know when your body is too overtaxed to fight off their temptations, enticements, and other worldly attractions. They know it is harder for you to resist their suggestions because everything seems natural and makes you feel good; this is your false reality.

These demons poison your soul further through your flawed thought process, broken will, hurt feelings, selfish desires, and negative emotions that bleed into your spirit. They wait patiently for your destructive inner thoughts, and then they whisper into your mind subtle remarks to stir you up and mislead you. They appeal to your innate desires by playing on your primitive human nature. Even though Satan's demons are clever, they are not the only things you should blame. Over your lifetime, your decisions have also significantly impacted your trinity. This impact includes even the foods you have selected for nourishment. Overindulgence in sugary and fried foods, along with too much coffee, are all associated with the stimulation of cortisol production. Your overly busy lifestyle has also contributed to chronically high cortisol levels. This over-stimulation of cortisol helps maintain your damaging core beliefs from past pains. This, in turn, can create insulin resistance, which leads to a deficiency in B vitamins, zinc, and magnesium (B vitamins are essential for cell metabolism and the maintenance of your central nervous system, brain, and spinal cord). Too much cortisol also promotes low levels of depression. Couple that with any negative or distorted thinking! Hopefully, you can grasp how your trinity works in unison and how one negative thought can wreak havoc within you.

AUTHOR'S WRITTEN PODCAST EPISODE 7: *"Be very careful, then, how you live—not as unwise but as wise..."* (Ephesians 5:15). Recapping: You are transformed by the renewal of your mind and through the power of the Holy Spirit. Everything you have experienced has shaped your thinking and altered who you were created to be (a reflection of Christ). The overproduction of cortisol brings edginess, over-reactions, negativity, worry, depression, anxiety, and other maladies. This imbalance causes your triune system to be out of sync, making you physically, emotionally, and spiritually weak. Our system was not created to cope with long-term chronic stimulation nor was it designed for a sedentary, socially isolated, indoor, sleep deprived, fast-pace, lifestyle. But there is hope if you are willing to *Change the Way You Change* by humbly submitting to God's authority from the inside out. (Let me warn you: if you are still talking after you have received God's Word, then your humility might not run very deep.) The Bible teaches in 1 Peter 5:6-11 and Romans 6 to guard your immaterial heart, yet the only way to control it is by the Holy Spirit. First, you need healthier internal principles to prevent and counter the production of your body's chemicals to grow toward the image of God. Then start *Changing the Way You Change* by achieving inner growth that will ignite the transforming power of the Holy Spirit. It is imperative to grasp the significance of your mental health as you examine your core beliefs. This book expresses that truth, honesty, faith, trust, obedience, and courage are the six areas you should grow in to become the "you" God created you to be to His glory. "*...since you have taken off your old self with its practices and have put on the new self, which is being renewed in knowledge in the image of its Creator.*" (Colossians 3:9-10).

WORKSTATION 5

If you always do
  What you always did,
You will always get
  What you already have,
A Dysfunctional You
—ADAPTED FROM JESSIE POTTER

The following is a list of emotions associated with eight sins that promote your soul to be stressed:

SADNESS: This emotion can consume you, steal your joy, and, left unchecked, will lead to self-destructive behavior.

GUILT: In a guilty state, your body cannot produce balanced chemicals. This emotion does not allow room for self-correction in large amounts, so that you can remain in its clutches for days and even years. It is easy to blame yourself or others, as it eats away at your insides. It can leave you with constant unhealthy remorse and feeling unloved, which leads to sadness and even depression.

FEAR: This emotion contradicts faith. Ask yourself, are your issues bigger than God? Is God not powerful enough to handle it? Has God told you the truth? Fear is Satan's tool to distract you; he wants you to forget about God's power. I am just asking, did Jesus not already defeat Satan on the cross? If you believe this, why are you listening to Satan?

ANGER: This emotion includes the heavyweights of wrath, hatred, fury, rage, resentment, irritation, and animosity. It is a selfish displeasure. Often, it is an emotional reaction to being hurt. It is interesting to know that anger, anxiety, and depression are the same basic emotions, with different behavioral manifestations that easily evolve into each other. Although anger is the most difficult of the three, underneath anxiety and depression is anger. Anger in and of itself is not sin, but becomes sinful when acted out unrighteously.

UNFORGIVENESS: This state of mind is a by-product of anger and selfishness. It instills deep hurt and resentment, destroying your peace and blocking your relationship with God. This is why God commands us to forgive.

GREED: This emotion is a form of idolatry, which leads to selfishness. It is linked to the root cause of theft, stinginess, and gluttony. It is said to be rooted in fear, based on a belief that you do not have enough or that you want more because your desires are not controlled.

PRIDE: This deceptive emotion often masks itself as false humility. Proverbs 8:13 tells us that pride is arrogant and evil. The manifestation of pride might sound like, "I can handle this," or "I do not need others or God to help with this small issue, so I do not need to seek advice or pray about it. I got this one." Or "I prayed about the situation, and I feel I should confront the person who hurt me." *"All a man's ways seem innocent to him, but motives are weighed by the Lord"* (Proverbs 16:2). *"For the word of God is alive and active... It judges the thoughts and attitude of the heart"* (Hebrews 4:12).

SELFISHNESS: This emotion is manipulative. Being self-centered can cause all kinds of emotional, mental, and physical sins. It sometimes manifests itself in the inability to see another person's point of view because you are full of your own desires. Stubbornness can be its companion. Selfish people can sometimes use God's commands to hurt others for their benefit or to prove they are right.

Self-reflections:

_____

_____

_____

_____

_____

_____

_____

_____

_____

_____

_____

_____

6

ATTITUDE ADJUSTMENT

The AA For A Healthier Perspective

The repetitiveness in this chapter is utilized not only to emphasize the intricate unity of our trinity but also to show the rippling effect throughout our body. Some research tells us that how we develop internally up to age 12 significantly and profoundly affects how we will be at age 32, physically, mentally, and emotionally. Again, because you live in a fallen world, it has altered who you were created to be. It also creates patterns of behaviors and beliefs mirrored by your body's chemistry that reflect the present-day you. Once more, who you are today is based on past thoughts and experiences that altered your body chemistry and directed you away from God. Any alteration to the harmony of your trinity has bred selfish ways of protecting yourself that led you, at a core level, to disregard God's truths. You then used worldly methods to meet bona fide needs, leaving you internally bruised. Even the act of unforgiveness bred feelings of anxiety that caused inappropriate and undesirable behaviors. Adjustments to your attitude are essential for any substantial change. If God is not controlling your life, who leads your existence, and by what methods? *"Do not conform any longer to the pattern of this world, but be transformed by the renewing of your mind. Then you will be able to test and approve what God's will is—his good, pleasing and perfect will"* (Romans 12:2).

God will not necessarily explain your pain and suffering; He has given you His promises and gifts. You cannot wait to see what God will do if you have not put the energy, effort, or time into obeying His Word. So, as you diligently and patiently wait for Him to answer your prayers, be sure your patience is grounded in your faith in Him. (Be advised that patience is a companion of wisdom.) Paul gave a glimpse into how to achieve victory in battle. It requires strict training to get the crown. You will experience real transformation when those things, people, and situations (aka "People, Places, and Things") that had you down can no longer keep you down. *"...Run in such a way as to get the prize. Everyone who competes in the games goes into strict training. They do it to get a crown that will not last, but we do it to get a crown that will last forever"* (1 Corinthians 9:24-25). *"Similarly, if anyone competes as an athlete, he does not receive the victor's crown unless he competes according to the rules"* (2 Timothy 2:5).

Living an internally secure life requires the reverse processing of your maladjusted cognitive mindset. This will bring harmony to your trinity and secure your relation to Christ. I emphasize that worldly passions circumvent God's created balance within your trinity. To live a life mentally attached to the contents of this world restricts you from realizing God's calling. Using Dr. Outley's analogy to stretch this point, the Earth is less than the size of a golf ball compared to the total universe. All your attachments to worldly things have caused you to expend your life's energy all for something the size of a golf ball. Dr. Outley assessed his problems as turmoil from old messes and internal dissatisfactions. He discovered that his psychological addictions had weakened his life over the years. Dr. Outley often stated that he perceived God's laws and principles as barriers and too restrictive. But he later realized those so-called barriers and restrictions are for our internal growth and, more importantly, the protection of His temple.

AUTHOR'S WRITTEN PODCAST EPISODE 8: As a teen, in my worldly mind, my existence came with restrictions imposed by the adult world. I could not do anything right in their eyes. If I did things their way, I was okay primarily until their way did not work. Even then, it was my fault. I developed some bitterness and exercised my will negatively, which was the only thing I could control. This newfound control veered me away from their teachings as I defiantly did things my way. I enjoyed the freedom to choose, but disliked any negative consequences, but my stubborn nature would not allow me to reveal my internal defeats. So, the willpower I exercised was only to demonstrate my capacity to make decisions that were the opposite of others. After years of exercising my authority over my life, two things were holding me back from experiencing God's freedom as a young Christian. 1) I had allowed my mind to become attached to this mundane world of people, places, and things as a way of surviving and establishing security. 2) I denied this attachment and convinced myself I was living faithfully in God's truth. *"Do not deceive yourselves. If any one of you thinks he is wise by the standards of this age, he should become a fool..."*

"... The Lord knows that the thoughts of the wise are futile"
(1 Corinthians 3:18, 20).

Dr. Outley also discovered that his negative thinking interfered with how his body metabolizes nutrients that sustain his trinity. He identified greed, lustful desires, self-centeredness, unforgiveness, entitlement, pride, impatience, fear, negativity, and expectations of others as some of his struggles and weaknesses. The breadth of those weaknesses allowed his spirit to seep through and out of his soul, leaving him internally bruised and bleeding. This left him ineffective at coping with life's issues. His body was out of balance as he habitually used his worldly cognitive processing to get relief. He then realized, in contrast, how constructive thoughts based on God's truths turned into optimistic feelings that elicited a positive attitude. This, in turn, aided his body in producing a balanced chemistry mixture for a healthier breakdown of nutrients so he could function optimally. To re-emphasize, you cannot use energy from your trinity in an imbalanced way without consequences. If the body is not sustained correctly, it cannot effectively react to stressors in its environment physically, mentally, or spiritually. The rippling effect of imbalance causes an adverse reaction, leading to more destructive results and internal imbalances—a damaging downward spiral. This ongoing vicious cycle within him could only be resolved by adopting a new philosophy that would produce healthy values. He eventually learned how to use his weaknesses to strengthen himself internally. Developing a value-driven perspective will support the balanced production of beneficial chemicals necessary to help you handle your present. Again, you need an honest look at your core beliefs using God's truths to reduce your emotional and social pathologies.

As Dr. Outley continued his journey to recalibrate his distorted core beliefs, he first accepted as truth that the Golden Rule (Matthew 7:12) was the map to feel secure and productive. He embedded the Golden Rule as the law of nature given by the Creator to bring balance to His creation. Even though the phrase "golden rule" is not found in the Bible, it is the name given to Jesus' teachings in the Sermon on the Mount—Matthew 5-7. The Golden Rule is a foundational structure for living. This foundation incorporates a blend of the physical, spiritual, biological, and psychological aspects within you. This blend is so integrated that it creates a harmonious union with effects not attainable by the summation of its parts. As you meditate on this, consider this inversion of the Golden Rule: *"So in everything, have others do to you what you do and have done to them."* Forgive my inherent nature, but a more positive summation is, *"so in everything, do to others what you secretly desire them to do to you."* The Golden Rule is the bridge from this life to an everlasting life with God. It will assist you as you clean out your internal messes, old and new.

The Golden Rule equips you to answer life's mysterious questions, such as: "Who am I?" "Why can't I find happiness?" "What is wrong with me?" "What is my purpose?" "What is love?" "What is true?" "Why is there so much pain?" "How can God love me?" "Can I change, etc.?"

If you are an extremely conservative Christian and find it challenging to live or worship with the differences of other people, let me say two things: 1) If a person is headed in the same direction (toward God), who are we to question their uniqueness. *"for whoever is not against us is for us."* Mark 9:40 & Matthew 12:30. 2) Perhaps the above question and thought can be answered as you transform from the inside out. Internalizing the Golden Rule will begin to heal many of your insecurities about yourself, other people, and the things of this world. *"So in everything, do to others what you would have them do to you, for this sums up the Law and the Prophets"* (Matthew 7:12).

AUTHOR'S WRITTEN PODCAST EPISODE 9: Our will is one of the most powerful gifts we receive from God, and may I say we wear it well. Our will is directed by our unreliable feelings, beliefs, and emotions based on experiences. No one can control their will or exercise this gift from God perfectly. Any confusion about this prevents us from feeling the peace of God's truth and grace. Be candid with yourself—the life God offers is what you find hard to receive. The life God offers has not been found because of your overindulgence in your primitive flesh. The world's poisons, Satan's manipulative tactics, and your experiences have left you with a worldly, empty life. Perhaps you can imagine how Satan has operated in your life, but can you also see the influences this world has had on your soul? The damage done to your soul and spirit in this world can be so subtle that it evades our detection. You have become so comfortable and accustomed to it that you do not see how this world's spirit is killing you physically, emotionally, mentally, and spiritually. Your worldly, created 'self' cannot experience harmony if ungodly thoughts chemically stimulate it. So, do not be fooled into thinking that your maladjusted skill set will get you further than where you are now. *"Above all else, guard your heart, for everything you do flows from it... keep corrupt talk far from your lips... Give careful thought to the paths for your feet and be steadfast in all your ways..."* (Proverbs 4:23-26—The Olive Tree Bible App. 2022).

As you know, your faith grows when you hear God's Word and obey it. And as you start to embrace His principles internally, your body will produce chemicals that cause a desire within you to act and react more positively. This turns your assent (agreed) faith toward saving faith. This one act must be followed by continual actions as you constantly hear God's truths with an internal belief. You will humbly grow and glow with integrity, esteem, confidence, faith, trust, courage, and other life-building powers. You can only change because of God's gifts and His plan for salvation. As you change with the power of the Spirit, be reminded that the gift of salvation is given through God's grace. When you earnestly do the internal work of self-cleansing and dying to self through Metanoia (repentance), you will actively participate in God's plan of salvation. God's grace teaches you to say no to sin (Titus 2:11-12); however, if God's gift of love and His grace do not compel you to change, perhaps you do not understand God's message, or maybe you have decided not to obey. Again, *Changing the Way You Change* begins with challenging your core beliefs and current values by measuring them against God's truths. When your heart accepts and acts on God's truths, it will foster a healthier core belief.

To demonstrate, take the computer analogy again: Imagine your computer is outdated and unable to continue its current operation because of old hardware that often breaks down or is slow to respond if it responds at all. It can only utilize updated software to operate more efficiently if newer hardware is installed. Any makeshift fixes only last for a brief time. The Golden Rule will be the hardware that brings balance and harmony to your trinity so that it can be reprogrammed to operate at its optimum level. With the Golden Rule hardware in place, your body can now download (utilize) God's message, the software program. A life aligned with God's principles will begin to establish such things as a sense of purpose, motivation, discipline, good mental health, obedience, endurance, faith, trust, courage, self-esteem, and self-control. Be mindful that this internal power and growth is not just about survival or your happiness. It is about living with an unshakable power governed by the principles of the Golden Rule. As you break the internal chains, the Golden Rule will allow you to program a healthier perspective. God has given us everything for a godly life, and whatever you need is already inside you; you need to choose and obey it, 1 Peter 4 and 2 Peter 1:3-4. Prayerfully, by now, you can understand why a new philosophy is warranted.

I'd like to offer you a glimpse into five aspects of Dr. Outley's philosophy. This philosophy is not meant to replace scriptural teachings but is built on a solid biblical foundation. Dr. Outley selectively merged research from psychology, biology, criminology, physiology, and biblical theology to create the Outleian Philosophy. It is a faith-based, applied clinical philosophy designed to modify cognitive distortions. At a core level, the Outleian Philosophy trusts what God has said with no doubts. An objective internal education of your spirituality leads to a mature, caring, and productive lifestyle. Education and training cannot change yesterday, but can help establish a different attitude and influence today and tomorrow. This change in attitude should lead you to examine your thinking patterns throughout the rest of your life.

SECONDLY: If applied honestly, the Outleian Philosophy will transport you from unhealthy habits to ones seeking God's approval. Dr. Outley taught that your inner self needs to conduct itself in love, respect, and faith with no doubts, selfish desires, or fears. I believe love and respect are the treasures you must store in heaven, which Jesus spoke about in Matthew 6:19-21. You must believe inwardly and demonstrate outwardly that God is this love, truth, and your ultimate reality. You can start your changing process with just one constructive thought because one positive thought can lead to habitual constructive thoughts when acted on consistently. Next, your body will begin to produce balanced chemicals. You will feel a difference when combined with proper nourishment and physical exercise. Your renewed philosophy, grounded in His truths, will assist you toward a soulish transformation. *"You stumble day and night, and the prophets stumble with you... My people are destroyed from a lack of knowledge. Because you have rejected knowledge, I also reject you...because you have ignored the law of your God"* (Hosea 4:5-6). *"All a man's ways seem innocent to him, but motives are weighed by the Lord."* (Proverb 16:2).

THIRDLY: The Outleian Philosophy is rooted in "you reap what you sow" along with *"...the measure you use, it will be measured to you."* (Luke 6:38). *"Do not be deceived... A man reaps what he sows"* (Galatians 6:7). *"As a man thinketh in his heart so is he"* (Proverb 23:7 KJV). It reflects the essential need to learn how to live, not just how to make a living. Dr. Outley's efforts to live within himself were centered on several biblical principles. These principles for living cannot corrode, be destroyed, or be corrupted. Your walk with God is not measured by merely following rules; after all, your sinful nature cannot measure up to God's standards. Even if you obeyed God's directions to the letter, it still would not be enough to earn salvation. His principles were not meant to become mindless laws for you to follow.

He gave them so you could become aware of your sin and how far you have strayed from Him. *"Therefore no one will be declared righteous in his sight by observing the law; rather, through the law we become conscious of sin"* (Romans 3:20).

FOURTHLY: The Outleian Philosophy also empowers you to reap the benefits of developing compassionate interest and concern for others. You are likely to use situations and circumstances to form perceptions to justify your actions or non-actions. This is not necessarily evil, but you have developed a philosophy that feeds your psychological addictions. Any negative thinking only serves to provide your distorted philosophy with more of an imbalance to create more messes. Your heart absorbed all this into a repressed reality for survival, to fit in and be accepted by others. You now justify your reactions with thoughts like, "That is just who I am," or "They needed to be told the truth," Or maybe you secretly lack forgiveness or goodwill toward others. All of this played out in the physical world as being the way things are as you took your eyes off God. Again, challenge your thoughts to adjust your attitude. This will foster positive thought patterns that align you closer to God's character. *"First clean the inside of the cup and dish, and then the outside also will be clean"* (Matthew 23:26). *"...Be kind and compassionate to one another, forgiving each other, just as in Christ God forgave you"* (Ephesians 4:32).

The final concept of the Outleian Philosophy recognizes that our five senses play a significant part in our internal dissatisfactions. Dr. Outley took a sober judgment of his external environment to determine how it had shaped his inner world of assets, deficits, and inadequate skills. He recognized how sin first came through Eve's senses. She first <u>heard</u> something contradictory to what God had said and entertained that thought. Eve's body chemistry was altered when she shifted her thoughts away from God's words. Next, she <u>saw</u> that the fruit was pleasing to her eyes. The fruit had to have felt good to her <u>touch</u> as she <u>smelled</u> its pleasant, intoxicating aroma. Four of her senses had been ignited; she was now fully intoxicated by her internal pharmacy of chemicals, as oxytocin, norepinephrine, serotonin, and dopamine flooded her system.

I need to stop and emphasize that these chemicals are your body's pleasure hormones. And a harmonious correlation exists as they support one another. Still, suppose your body produces too much or too little of these chemicals. In that case, it can cause damaging symptoms such as paranoia, confusion, restlessness, attention deficit, impulsive behaviors, and a desire for instant gratification. For example, an overproduction of oxytocin—the so-called love hormone—can make you oversensitive to other people, proving detrimental. If Eve's body were now changing the production of these hormones and neurotransmitters, I imagine she would become anxious and confused with an impulsive need for instant gratification. With four of her senses triggered, Satan entrapped her with her internal desires and perspective. She had never been in this situation before and failed to return to her Creator to regain internal stability. She was entrapped, triggered, and thus unable internally to resist her lustful desire to please herself. So, she indulged in her sinful nature and <u>tasted</u> the forbidden fruit.

Once the sin was committed, this raised their cortisol levels as fear, anxiety, paranoia, agitation, guilt, and shame were evoked. They did not recognize the need for their Creator, and their souls became independent as they tried to protect themselves the best way they knew. This was evidenced by their desire to cover their naked bodies as they hid from God. They were not only naked on the outside (physically), but they were spiritually and emotionally naked as well. The consequences of this one act, instigated by one thought, changed them and their entire family's lives. The harmony of their created trinity was chemically altered, even affecting their unborn children. As such, they had lost favor and certain privileges with their Creator because they did not repent or ask for forgiveness. You can only imagine their mindset based on some of your own experiences.

Your present philosophy was solidified through your five senses. This occurred as you were being manipulated by the instinctive nature of your body's needs for survival, security, and pleasures. Our brain is also hard-wired to seek out behaviors that release dopamine in our reward system. When doing pleasurable things, your brain produces a large amount of dopamine. You feel good, and you seek to have more of those feelings. This may be why junk food and sugar are so addictive. But this neurotransmitter is more about wanting than liking. So, when we hear, see, touch, smell, and taste pleasing things, they are not necessarily beneficial for our trinity. Subconsciously, any hidden guilt or shame can create a self-protective psychological mask. Again, your cheerful obedience and consistent efforts to get to know Christ will prompt your body to produce more balanced chemistry. This is how and when you become a new creation. Transformation is not a one-time event; it is much more than just a belief in God. Your faith, continually exercised by your free will, changes you to be more like Christ. God wants a relationship with you and desires you to enjoy one with Him. God's plan of salvation was to rescue you from your sinful nature to a restored relationship with Him. *"Set your minds on things above, not on earthly things"* (Colossians 3:2).

"...You have taken off your old self with its practices and have put on the new self, which is being renewed in knowledge in the image of its Creator" (Colossians 3:9-10). Based on the information you have received thus far, there is a good chance you have been overwhelmed. Your senses are being overstimulated not only by technology and the busyness of this world but also by the necessity to change. Although you are prone to the sin of this world, like the prodigal son, you can make a repentant return and achieve tremendous mental and spiritual growth on this side of Heaven. Once again, this is accomplished by building God's truths into your physiology. Submitting to His leadership changes and transforms your soul. Be encouraged that when God gives you a command, He also gives you the power to carry it out. When you are centered in faith, you gain the power of the Holy Spirit and the ability to understand, honor, and obey God. As stated, you must continually strive to keep your mind and dependence on the Lord, not just verbally but behaviorally. *"For sin shall no longer be your master, because you are not under the law, but under grace"* (Romans 6:14).

AUTHOR'S WRITTEN PODCAST EPISODE 10: *"If you love me, you will obey what I command. And I will ask the Father, and he will give you another Counselor to be with you forever... If anyone who loves me, he will obey my teachings. My Father will love him, and we will come to him and make our home with him"* (John 14:15-16, 23). Salvation is the centerpiece of your spiritual connection to and with God. To be with God, you must walk the salvation road to the end of your earthly existence. He plans to get Himself into you, and it is not the result of anything mechanically you do or have done. The grace God is giving encompasses more than His unmerited mercy or favor. With your faith, you will activate God's grace with unquestionable confidence and no doubts concerning His promises. As your faith connects you with an active submission to God, His grace allows you to enjoy this life's wonders freely. Your saving faith will continue to seek greater truth and knowledge.

Simply put, it saves your soul from the power and effects of your sins. This form of faith is credited as righteousness and viewed as works in sanctification. *"...The righteous will live by faith"* (Romans 1:17).

Sanctification is you being made holy, purified, and set apart for God's special purpose. When He purchased forgiveness on the cross, Jesus' blood washed and sanctified you. So, as a saint, you enjoy His daily purification from the evil that separates (not isolates) you from this world. *"... Let us purify ourselves from everything that contaminates body and spirit, perfecting holiness out of reverence for God"* (2 Corinthians 7:1). *"...so that, just as sin reigned in death, so also grace might reign through righteousness to bring eternal life through Jesus Christ our Lord"* (Romans 5:21). Ask yourself if the faith you have today is sufficient to spiritually sustain you for the rest of your life on earth. Your faith should be growing and leading you, daily, moment by moment, to a better understanding of the things of God and to greater levels of obedience, which will transform your soul. Your active submission to His will allows your confidence to grow as you walk daily with God.

Changing the Way You Change will be that continuous walk with God as you are being transformed from within. Once more, the only way to salvation is by God's gift of grace that He offers freely to you. But like any gift, you must receive, open, wear, and display the gift to show your appreciation. You receive God's gift of grace by your active faith, you open and accept His gift by believing and studying His Word, and you display and wear His gift humbly, yet proudly, by obeying His Word as you let your heart be continually filled with the Holy Spirit. If you do not accept God's gift, it is left wrapped, unopened, and unappreciated. When that happens, you never actually get the benefit of the gift! *"You need to persevere so that when you have done the will of God, you will receive what he has promised"* (Hebrews 10:36).

The above is nothing less than a continual active devotion, commitment, and vow to God. There is no salvation without your faith. There is no faith without your heart's desire for active obedience. With God's gifts and your free will, you can now take your faith in God and demonstrate your appreciation. Your free will enables you to believe or deny God's authority, as did Satan and his demons. They disqualified themselves from receiving His gifts. Once you are participating in God's plan for salvation, it can save you from the control that sin has in your life by the power of the Holy Spirit living in you. Submit to Christ and clean His house so He can actively dwell within you. Although there is only one way to participate in God's plan of salvation, there are three phases associated with salvation:

JUSTIFICATION is the past tense of salvation. It means to accept and treat as justified. Justification vindicated you. You were saved from the penalties of sin because you trusted in

Christ. It settled the legal status of your position before God. As you navigate *Changing the Way You Change*, digging deeper into God's Word is vital to embrace a richer insight into His plan for salvation. God's Word aims to keep His saints from being deprived of future salvation. *"I have been crucified with Christ and I no longer live, but Christ lives in me. The life I now live in the body, I live by faith in the Son of God, who loved me and gave himself for me. I do not set aside the grace of God...."* (Galatians 2:20-21).

SANCTIFICATION is the present tense of salvation. You are presently saved from sin's power over you. You can learn to live the Christian life daily, enabling you to make character changes as your soul is transforming. You are being made holy, set apart for God's use. Conforming to Christ's image and moral attributes is a daily, moment-by-moment process. *"Sanctify them by the truth: your word is truth"* (John 17:17). *"Since we have these promises, dear friends, let us purify ourselves from everything that contaminates body and spirit, perfecting holiness out of reverence for God"* (2 Corinthians 7:1).

GLORIFICATION is the future tense of salvation and God's final removal of sin. You are saved from sin's presence and cannot sin when you receive your new body. *"I consider that our present sufferings are not worth comparing with the glory that will be revealed in us"* (Romans 8:18). *"For our light and momentary troubles are achieving for us an eternal glory that far outweighs them all"* (2 Corinthians 4:17).

Hopefully, you are encouraged to dig deeper into God's Word. I encourage you to study these five words associated with His plan for salvation:

A. Faith
B. Grace
C. Redemption
D. Deliverance
E. Purification

To help jumpstart your effort, I will reiterate the first two, faith and grace. But before getting started, meditate on these scriptures to feed your soul. *"...Those he called, he also justified; those he justified, he also glorified"* (Romans 8:30). *"Who have been chosen according to the foreknowledge of God the Father, through the sanctifying work of the Spirit, for obedience to Jesus Christ..."* (1 Peter 1:2). *"But we ought always to thank God for you, brothers loved by the Lord, because from the beginning God chose you to be saved through the sanctifying work of the spirit and through belief in the truth."* (2 Thessalonians 2:13).

1. Your active obedience demonstrates your faith, thereby becoming a saving faith. Your heart's desire should start with your mental and physical obedience to God's Word. The power of the Holy Spirit working in you will aid your heart's desire to obey God and deter you from returning to your former sinful nature. This obedience will be a continuous soulish transformation through Him and for His name's sake *"...to the obedience that comes from faith"* (Romans 1:5). 2. Your faith activates His grace. You are saved by God's grace through your will to exercise your trust in Him. With your active faith, His grace

gives you the gift of salvation. *"For it is by grace you have been saved, through faith—and this is not from yourselves, it is the gift of God—not by works, so that no one can boast"* (Ephesians 2:8-9). *"...we have gained access by faith into this grace in which we now stand"* (Romans 5:2).

To dismiss any resistance you might have, let me remind you that by your faith in Christ, you have the power of the Holy Spirit to control the entities of your soul, including your emotions. Although the emotional part of you is instrumental, at other times, it is highly counterproductive. Remember, subconscious and conscious emotions are automatically and chemically stimulated. Either way, they are hard to control, and when they are intense, they can provoke you. Again, it does not matter if your emotions are rational; they prompt you toward an action of some kind. Your body's chemicals associated with those emotions can build up over time and become explosive. Maturing your soul is vital as you learn how to take control of your emotions by aligning your thoughts with Christ's. *"...Take captive every thought to make it obedient to Christ."* (2 Corinthians 10:5).

A quick illustration using three emotions: anger, love, and fear. Anger can stimulate healthy competition toward success, or you can ignite it into rage, resentment, envy, or fury. Or you can control anger with God's truths. Now, take the emotion of love; if you are honest, it can be possessively destructive to you and another person. In that case, it ignites negative thoughts that trigger adverse chemicals. And lastly, fear can be highly destructive to your body, soul, and spirit. Fear is an unpleasant emotion caused by the perception of danger that alerts you to react. The perception of fear can be real, imagined, physical, or emotional. Living with an unfounded fear of people, places, or things will cause you to develop an unhealthy perspective.

It changes the way your body functions, which affects your behavior. Unfounded fear can be reflected in your behavior or attitude even when you logically know it is baseless. *"Fear of man will prove to be a snare, but whoever trusts in the Lord is kept safe"* (Proverbs 29:25).

Author's Written Podcast Episode 11: Wrapping Up! The world has confused you via your innate lustful desires, experiences, and emotionally produced body chemicals. Humans have become so confused by all the enticements of this world that it is difficult to understand what is what. Dr. Outley explained man's confusion as being those bright and glittery parts of the world that captivate and throw your senses into overstimulation. *"Do not store up for yourselves treasures on earth, where moths and rust destroy, and where thieves break in and steal. But store up for yourselves treasures in heaven... for where your treasure is there your heart will be also"* (Matthew 6:19-21). *"Do your best to present yourself to God as one approved, a worker who does not need to be ashamed and who correctly handles the word of truth"* (2 Timothy 2:15).

As described earlier, transformation's real power is in the Golden Rule's internalization. To want the absolute best for another person is authentic. Suppose you could take a part of yourself to honestly want the best for others, despite their dysfunctional behavior or your bad mood. This could create a robust reciprocal process where others can experience God's love through you. Prayerfully, they, too, can begin to work toward a better self. Nonetheless, it would leave you with an untouchable sense of humble confidence in all aspects of your life. This effort would generate an internal pattern of godly habits, promoting a balanced mixture of body chemicals. This would also be beneficial in detaching from the physical world so you can attach to God's power in a more excellent way. Are you living in a world of dying things, or are you dying to yourself to reach the living? My observation is: after confessing our faith in Christ, we cannot rebuild what we tore down—our old shack of a life. As we are being transformed, consider yourself as that spiritual being having a human experience, thus having the power of the Holy Spirit to affect the course of human events. Now, visualize the spiritual aspect of you having that human experience.

WORKSTATION 6

Consider these strategies as you battle old core beliefs to recalibrate, changing your attitude and developing healthier principles.

Refrain from overwhelming or overloading yourself. Start with one at a time and work your way down the list. If you disagree with or are unwilling to follow these suggestions, put the whole thing away. You are probably not ready to look at your psychological addictions and heal yourself internally. That is okay, but be aware that you will continue to do what you have always done and realize the exact results you already have.

1. Be honest with yourself—do you know the difference between facts and truths? Do you also recognize that your opinions, education, experiences, feelings, and perceptions are not the standard?

   Your thoughts now:

   _____

   _____

   _____

   _____

   Your thoughts after praying and meditating:

   _____

   _____

   _____

   _____

2. Do you accept that life includes boredom, passion, depression, and grief? Have your dysfunctional ways of coping with them erased any of them?

Your thoughts now:

_____

_____

_____

_____

Your thoughts after praying and meditating:

_____

_____

_____

_____

3. Are you tolerant of people's mistakes and ignorance, including your own?

Your thoughts now:

_____

_____

_____

_____

Your thoughts after praying and meditating:

_____

_____

_____

_____

4. When responding to situations and circumstances, are you controlled by God rather than your innate, chemically induced emotions?

Your thoughts now:

_____

_____

_____

_____

Your thoughts after praying and meditating:

_____

_____

_____

_____

5. What will you do to slow down and concentrate on the present rather than the past to work toward your eternal future?

Your thoughts now:

_____

_____

_____

_____

Your thoughts after praying and meditating:

_____

_____

_____

_____

6. What are you doing to keep yourself in good spiritual and physical health? And how is it transforming your soul?

   Your thoughts now:

   _____

   _____

   _____

   _____

   Your thoughts after praying and meditating:

   _____

   _____

   _____

   _____

7. What positive life management skills are you developing, and what are you doing that is helping you move in a positive direction toward salvation?

   Your thoughts now:

   _____

   _____

   _____

   _____

   Your thoughts after praying and meditating:

   _____

   _____

   _____

   _____

8. Do you look back with regret and do not look forward with fear? Just look around yourself with complete awareness. Learn to listen to the Holy Spirit from within by having a quiet, meditative time with Him.

    Your thoughts now:

    _____
    _____
    _____
    _____

    Your thoughts after praying and meditating:

    _____
    _____
    _____
    _____

9. Are you learning to forgive your internal wounds, and are you content that your forgiveness does not always achieve reconciliation?

    Your thoughts now:

    _____
    _____
    _____
    _____

    Your thoughts after praying and meditating:

    _____
    _____
    _____
    _____

10. Do you fully understand God's plan for salvation and His truths?

Your thoughts now:

_____

_____

_____

_____

Your thoughts after praying and meditating:

_____

_____

_____

_____

11. What are you doing to get a better understanding of God's plan? And is it working for you?

_____

_____

_____

_____

_____

_____

_____

_____

_____

_____

_____

7

CLEANSING THE SOUL

As alluded to earlier and based on 30-plus years in the mental health field, I believe most of the negative emotions we are experiencing today are the residual pains and crumbs left over from unforgiveness. You buried these lingering pains internally, which were never fully resolved. Pushing through the shame and fears of being hurt again, you hid, shielded your pain, licked your wounds, and allowed them to fester as you tried to get on with life. You are only trying to fix yourself with old skills and outdated internal information as you maneuver through life using only your five senses. Destructive self-talk causes your body to be depleted of vital substances, energy, and adrenaline hormones to deal properly with your present-day stress. Thus far, your endeavors have been ineffective in controlling your flesh and soul cravings. Go ahead and test your perspective and self-talk against God's truth.

You have looked for God in all the wrong places to make

sense of your worldly life. You may even find yourself stuck in one of life's transitions with no internal growth toward salvation. You can make smooth life transitions by letting go of what is behind you and beginning something fresh daily. As your fleshly body grows and matures, it will naturally deteriorate due to stress from the wear and tear of people, places, and things you experience. However, negative core beliefs can accelerate the deterioration process.

Although you may have subconsciously suppressed the truth and denied God's authority, there is hope. So be encouraged because there is no shame in who you have become, even with your messes, issues, and faults, but understand who you have become compared to who you were created to be. As the higher intellectual creature God created you to be, you can acquire knowledge to build on your faith. God is ready and waiting for your actions to be transformed toward Him. As already pointed out, a soulish person is led by the spirit.

Again, being weighed down with worldly things has caused your trinity to be altered. Once freed from past burdens and faulty thinking, you can begin to transform your soul. Remember, you are equipped with everything you need to be productive in your endeavor to change. First, start by unpacking what God has packed inside you; use it to expose the roots of your hurtful memories, worldly imprinted learning, and ungodly habits that have weighed you down and caused all types of dysfunctions.

Let me give you another snippet of how my mind created additional stress. My understanding of the New Testament did not fit into my worldly concept of life. When I read words and phrases full of His grace and spirit, boldness, perseverance, faithful, obedient, etc., I already felt a sense of mental, spiritual, emotional, and physical defeat. In my mind, I concluded that God did not create me that way, and I questioned why. My trinity at that moment produced chemicals that offset its balance based on that thought. This illogical, negative, self-defeating thought did not motivate me mentally to get up and do what was needed to glorify Christ. I wanted to wallow in my negative thinking and say, "What is the use?" "I am doing my best," or "This is just who I am."

I had no idea what was deep inside my heart and soul from past hurts and experiences. This kept my body in a disheartened state. But as those hard places around my heart got chipped away, I finally realized I was allowing my mind to conjure up and charm old attitudes about myself and others. My body's chemistry was causing this inability to gain a healthier outlook. After realizing what was happening, I prayed, meditated, and allowed the Holy Spirit to lead me. I could now take a different, more constructive path. It then occurred to me that by God's grace, I had some knowledge and resources to take care of my physical body, and to a limited degree, I understood how to aid my spiritual walk. However, I was left questioning how to care for my soul. Again, this is where I believe our most profound needs go unmet and keep us from fully experiencing God, and why our transformation stagnates. My soul and spirit were not made from the earth like my body, but placed in me by our Creator. So, I genuinely believe my soul is the only part of my trinity needing transformation and salvation. *"And the dust returns to the ground it came from and the spirit returns to God who gave it."* (Ecclesiastes 12:7).

God gave you a plethora of knowledge, the act of forgiveness, a heart to understand, and His laws to live by for a reason. I am confident that forgiving is one of His most fundamental laws. Forgiveness is God's way of responding to some of life's pain that will release you from the internal torment that unforgiveness produces. Yes, it is okay to feel feelings and express them. After all, you were created with a range of emotions. Even so, suppose they are leading you to display dysfunctional and unproductive behavior that does not glorify God. In that case, remaining stuck in this self-defeating, self-destructive mode is unacceptable. The goal throughout your lifespan is growth that transforms you. This is not just about learning to live with undesirable feelings. It is a heart issue that promotes good mental health, which is not the absence of mental illness. It is the ability to cope with daily life and its challenges by having the courage and confidence to make changes that glorify Him, even when it is uncomfortable or painful.

Forgiveness will set you up to handle all sorts of maladjustments in your inner life as it allows your body to produce an array of vital chemicals with proper nutrition, exercise, and rest. Our trinity works together in complex ways, much of which is unbeknownst to us. I want to stretch your thinking again by saying you cannot work on one area of your trinity without working on the other two areas simultaneously with the same compassion. What is the use of feeding your body nutritionally if your negative thinking does not allow you to digest it properly? What is the use of reading your Bible daily if your heart is not moved to accept and experience God's grace? What is the use of you saying you have faith if your heart is not moved to act on or share it?

Once more, nothing in our trinity works in isolation. Forgiveness is a cleanser for the soul. Forgiveness is a choice of your will.

The following study and seven principles for healing are being offered to help you cleanse your soul. They are based on a concept I heard from Dr. Chuck Swindoll's radio ministry.

FORGIVENESS

The Soul Cleanser

"In him we have redemption through his blood, the forgiveness of sins, in accordance with the riches of God's grace that he lavished on us with all wisdom and understanding" (Ephesians 1:7-8).

PRAYER: "God, I thank you for the opportunity to share your Word. Let the Holy Spirit teach and help us to obey your word. We ask for forgiveness for our hidden faults, those things we take for granted, and those that we ignore. Please keep us from willful sin as You protect us from ourselves. May our negative thoughts not rule over us. Protect our hearts and give us hearts that are pleasing to You. Grant us a willing spirit to honor and glorify You, not to sustain us. God, you know where we hurt. Thus, we ask that you direct us to the pains and hurts to identify and bring them into the light. We know that you know how they can be fixed, and we ask You to guide our process toward healing. You know our limits and all our efforts, regardless of the process. So, we also ask and invite you to do your healing work within us. We give our wills freely over to You to do as You will. God, we pray also that you are pleased with this temple you live in within us. We pray all of this and more in Jesus' great name. Amen, Amen."

Start cleansing by meditating on these scriptures, which will guide your heart and thoughts and prepare you for *Changing the Way You Change.*

HOSEA 4:6— *"My people are destroyed from lack of knowledge."*

ROMANS 2:13— *"It is not the hearers of the law who are just before God, but the doers of the law will be justified."*

CORINTHIANS 6:12— *"I have the right to do anything, you say—but not everything is beneficial."*

CHRONICLES 7:14— *"If my people, who are called by my name, will humble themselves and pray and seek my face and turn from their wicked ways, then will I hear from heaven and will forgive their sin...."*

PSALM 103:11-17— *"For as high as the heavens are above the earth, so great is his love for those who fear him; as far as the east is from the west, so far how he removed our transgressions from us. As a father has compassion on his children, so the Lord has compassion on those who fear him; for he knows how we are formed, he remembers that we are dust... The Lord's love is with those who fear him, and his righteousness with their children's children—with those who keep his covenant and remember to obey his precepts."*

PROVERBS 16:2— *"All a person's ways seem pure to them, but motives are weighed by the Lord."*

Forgiveness is used over 140 times in the Bible. So, I consider it a fundamental principle God has given us. It means to let go and cancel a debt, offense, or sin done to you.

In my line of work, I have learned that what most people have been taught about forgiveness is nothing more than a type of suppression from the emotional pains they encountered.

Psychologically, choosing to forgive and let something go does not work very well. Although you say you forgive, and it is consciously forgotten, the pain associated with it is stored in your subconscious. When you overreact to present situations, it is usually because of suppressed pain from past hurts. When something is suppressed for years, it can become hate-related symptoms of resentment, shame, blaming others, bitterness, and criticalness. You may not be consciously aware, but it is slowly altering your body's chemistry. Unforgiveness can bring subtle hostility, resentment, and destruction to the spirit, none of which reflect God's character. Although you try to mask and shield your pain, it is only being suppressed deeper, wreaking profound havoc internally.

Consider this old saying, "You feel what you believe, or you believe what you feel." Be aware that your body's need for emotional stability, security, and love has trumped any logic you tried to counter your pain with most of the time. As a human, it is not natural to forgive because all you want to do is retaliate or withdraw to focus on your wounds. Your mind holds firm to the injustice done to you, consciously and/or subconsciously. This can create a level of distortion in your life and motivation. It can cause you to come across as harsh, intimidating, weak, insensitive, or overly sensitive. While some become stuck in this destructive whirlwind, in others, it can create a dullness with doubts about your identity. You develop a knack for behaving as if things are okay in front of others. However, when alone, your demons bring out your fears and insecurities as you isolate yourself with negative thoughts. This alters your current mood, behavior, character, and personality through the over- or under-production of the body's chemicals.

ILLUSTRATION: Think of it this way: unforgiveness is food (unforgiveness = food) that you ate that became stuffed and stuck deep in your body (suppressed). Now that unforgiveness/food is never released by the body, it begins to rot, creating worms, gases, and foul odors. The gas from the fermentation process begins to break down your physical body and its organs. This is how unforgiveness works. One of the gases of unforgiveness, metaphorically speaking, is resentment, which breaks down your soul with destructive behaviors, negative thinking, overreactions, anxiety, and unwarranted fear. You begin to feel sick physically, mentally, emotionally, and spiritually, without knowing the root cause. To release the suppressed resentment and pain, you must bring your body back to a state of well-being; you need a body cleanser. A colonoscopy is one of the physical diagnostic tools that doctors use to prevent cancer or other illnesses from taking hold.

Forgiveness is the spiritual/biblical tool used as a soul cleanser. It releases all that psychologically rotten stuff inside you to begin healing. It can also be a preventive method, warding off future breakdowns in your body. You need forgiveness in your day-to-day life; however, you also need it for your memories. Again, let me elaborate on why. Trash left over from old messes creates a fertile breeding ground for new messes. Everything you have experienced has helped shape your core beliefs, which, along with imbalanced body chemistry, sparked your maladjusted behavior. Forgiveness is God's way of responding to some of life's emotional pain, which releases you from the torment of unforgiveness and allows Him to work in your life, thus creating a more balanced chemistry.

FORGIVENESS

Matthew 18:21-35

Then Peter came to Jesus and asked, "Lord, how many times shall I forgive my brother or sister who sins against me? Up to seven times?" Jesus answered, "I tell you, not seven times, but seventy-seven times. "Therefore, the kingdom of heaven is like a king who wanted to settle accounts with his servants. As he began the settlement, a man who owed him ten thousand talents was brought to him. Since he was not able to pay, the master ordered that he and his wife and his children and all that he had be sold to repay the debt. "At this the servant fell on his knees before him. 'Be patient with me,' he begged, 'and I will pay back everything.' The servant's master took pity on him, canceled the debt, and let him go.

"But when that servant went out, he found one of his fellow servants who owed him a hundred silver coins. He grabbed him and began to choke him. 'Pay back what you owe me!' he demanded. "His fellow servant fell to his knees and begged him, 'Be patient with me, and I will pay it back.' "But he refused. Instead, he went off and had the man thrown into prison until he could pay the debt. When the other servants saw what had happened, they were outraged and went and told their master everything that had happened.

"Then the master called the servant in. 'You wicked servant,' he said, 'I canceled all that debt of yours because you begged me to. Shouldn't you have had mercy on your fellow servant just as I had on you?' In anger his master handed him over to the jailers to be tortured, until he should pay back all he owed. This is how my heavenly Father will treat each of you unless you forgive your brother or sister from your heart."

PRINCIPLE 1: The King called his servants to give an account of what was owed. You cannot forgive a debt you do not know the actual amount. You cannot wholly forgive the offense until you see what was done to you, the extent of the damage and hurt, and how it made you feel.

In my profession, I have assessed that people commonly bury their emotional pain to avoid feeling it, or they fly off the handle as a guard toward self-protection. However, they almost always resurface in other ways. You first learned to use this defense mechanism as a child to stop feeling any emotional pain. You were probably told to push the bad feelings down and forget about them. Nevertheless, your mind does not forget; it has simply relocated that memory outside your conscious reality. Eventually, when something in the present looks remotely like it, your mind will use that past distorted information to filter present situations. You are left overreacting in the present based on residual pain from past hurts.

PRINCIPLE 2: The servant had a wife and children. He lived on a slave's wages. He did not have the means to repay the billions he owed. The one who caused the pain to you does not have the means to repay the offense or remove the pain from your life.

When you are wounded, you will often look to your offender or abuser for repayment. However, when you seek resolution or restitution from those responsible for your original wound, you will almost always be disappointed. No one can address those wounds and remove your pain because they are too great for man to handle. The only remedy is God's renewal. Only the truth from the Holy Spirit can calm your painful past if you submit your will to His and allow Him to heal your wounds.

PRINCIPLE 3: When the King realized the severity of the situation, he reacted angrily and commanded that the servant, his wife, children, and all he had be sold for repayment. The emotion of anger is a normal and sometimes healthy response. But this servant's apparent irresponsible behavior was totally disrespectful to the King. How the servant could have gotten into so much debt is difficult to comprehend. He owed billions of dollars, living on a slave's wages! But the King knew the money was gone and would never get it back.

You may have been told that anger is sinful, while others instruct their children not to express it. Yet Ephesians 4:26 states: *"In your anger, do not sin."* So, you can be angry for moral reasons. Anger becomes a sin when dwelt on, worried about, and acted upon unrighteously. Paul also describes how sinful anger originates in the last half of that verse and the one that follows it: *"Do not let the sun go down while you are still angry, and do not give the devil a foothold."* Satan wants you to dwell on your anger daily; he wants you to lick your wounds but not do anything about them. He also wants you to turn your anger inward and bury it deeply so that when something else happens that is remotely like the original offense, his demonic forces will take the opportunity to stir you up so you will react inappropriately in the present. He knows your past hurts and core beliefs. He is appealing to those past emotions associated with your faulty and distorted thinking. He also knows you did not develop a mature soul that is being transformed daily to withstand his lies. Satan is appealing to the emotional you. Again, God did not create you to be emotionally driven because your emotions lack the spiritual substance from God's truth. All your time and energy have been wasted on past things you cannot control or correct, except to release them.

When it comes to your anger, it must be identified, internally dealt with, and released by willfully surrendering it to Jesus. Once this is done, ask yourself what purpose it has. Why do you need to hold on to it? And when you are emotionally ready to release it, let God know that you give it to Him freely because you do not need it; you do not want it, nor do you want it back.

PRINCIPLE 4: At first glance, it seems the servant had come to some repentance, but when he promised to repay everything, he lied to protect himself, which revealed a heart of deceit. He had run up an enormous debt, and he knew he could never pay it back nor, I believe, intended to do so. He was a thief through irresponsible behavior. (Just a tidbit on this humongous debt: ten thousand talents are 200,000 years of labor, which is sixty million working days. In our day and time, it is approximately 3.48 billion dollars.

You often offer forgiveness contingent on the attitude and integrity of the person you are forgiving. But genuine forgiveness has nothing to do with the perspective of the one being forgiven. Forgiveness is not dependent on the person wanting or asking for it. Forgiveness is cutting off, releasing, or sending away the offense done to you, whether the offender has a change of heart or not.

The word "forgiveness" focuses on the offense and the wrong that was done to you, not the one who did the wrong. *"If we confess our sins, he is faithful and just and will forgive us our sins and purify us from all unrighteousness"* (1 John 1:9). The focus of forgiveness is on the sin, not the sinner. The sin receives the action of the verb forgive. God releases and cuts off the sin, not the sinner. You do not want God to cut you off, but you want Him to free you from your sins and debts to purify you.

"'Forgive us our debts as we also have forgiven our debtors. And lead us not into temptation but deliver us from the evil one.' If you forgive others when they sin against you, your heavenly Father will forgive you. But if you do not forgive others their sins, your Father will not forgive your sins" (Matthew 6:12-15).

PRINCIPLE 5: In verse 27, the King felt compassion, released the servant, and forgave the debt. You cannot forgive while still feeling the offense's pain; forgiveness will be almost impossible. However, you need to follow your pain to its core belief and align it with God's truth so that the pain of the offense can be brought to light. You can release the offense when the pain is gone and replaced with peace and compassion. Sympathy says I feel sorry for you, but compassion says, I know the pain you carry, for I, too, have carried a similar burden.

The King's compassion exposed his sincere heart and belief system. Compassion is the benevolent action and emotional identification you can make with the one who offended you. When you come into the truth and receive God's grace of forgiveness, you can see the person who hurt you from God's perspective. You can identify with the offender as a fellow sinner who also needs forgiveness. You can forgive when you see in that person, to some degree, that which is also present in yourself. Let me elaborate; if you were physically abused, you might have never abused anyone else in that way, but you have offended or abused in other ways. The pain and emotional scars are there. Pain is pain, and no one can say that one person's pain is more significant than another's. We are all different and internalize things in diverse ways. The intensity of someone's pain is not necessarily correlated to the offense.

In Romans 2:1, Paul writes: *"You, therefore, have no excuse, you who pass judgment on someone else, for at whatever point you judge another, you are condemning yourself, because you who pass judgment do the same things. "* So go ahead and cast the first stone. However, when you come into the truth God has for you and receive His peace, you can experience the release from the need for revenge and, thus, cut off the offense and truly forgive.

PRINCIPLE 6: Notice the two contrasting statements in verses 27 and 28; the King released, canceled, and let him go, but the servant in verse 28 seized, grabbed, and choked. The King became free internally from being emotionally attached to the stress of maintaining the note, his pain, and his anger. On the other hand, the servant was still in bondage to his evil heart. As such, he seized, grabbed, and held onto his fellow worker. This shows that he was still holding onto his pain and anger.

In Matthew 18, Jesus wanted Peter to understand that forgiveness frees the forgiver. The person who caused the trouble for Peter needed to be forgiven so that Peter could be free. Peter's genuine concern was how long he had to carry his resentment, frustration, and internal pain. I think Jesus suggested that if Peter looked long enough at the offender, he might find something identifiable.

Forgiveness can change only the one doing the forgiving, not necessarily the one being forgiven. You can be emotionally freed from other people and their behavior, whether they ever change or not. Other people's behavior does not have the power to control you emotionally. However, I understand that your experiences can appear more potent than the logical truth of the present. Your actions, reactions, and inactions will demonstrate your core beliefs. Remember, your thought process is producing adverse chemicals in your body. I ask, is your situation too great

CHANGING THE WAY YOU CHANGE

for God to handle? Do you really believe your response from your core was righteous?

If Peter had forgiven his offender 77 times, he would still be in the same place he had started if he had not found freedom from his emotional connection with his offender. The number of times you forgive will not be determined by whether the person who has offended you will act differently in the future. When you forgive, you must do so without expectations that the person being forgiven will change or be able to restore your pain or repay a debt. If you are willing to let go from a heart level, God can replace your pain with His perfect peace. In Hebrew and according to religious numerology, 77 symbolizes completion or perfection, and 7 communicates a sense of fullness or completeness. (Fun Tidbits: when added together, the numerical position of each letter in CHRIST equals 77. In Psalm 77, the psalmist shows a great change of mood when he begins to remember, meditate, and consider God's works, goodness, and power. He has lifted his eyes from himself to the Lord. Lastly, the number 7 appears over 700 times in the Bible.

LETTER	NUMERICAL POSITION
C	3
H	8
R	9
I	18
S	19
T	20
TOTAL	**77**

PRINCIPLE 7: We know the King and the servant never became friends because the scripture says the servant was handed over to be tortured until the debt was paid in full. Living on slave wages meant he did not have the means to repay this huge debt, nor could he offer compensation if he were tortured daily. Physically, he was unable to work and was condemned with no hope.

This passage shows well the consequences of unforgiveness, being turned over to your inner agony, and the torment of faulty thinking. This has allowed Satan's demons like Shame, Guilt, Depression, Loneliness, Stress, Insecurity, Fear, and Bitterness, along with your feelings of emptiness, to come in and set up shop in God's temple. You are being tormented daily by reliving the past with less energy to live for today. This can waste years of your life by sapping energy and vitality from your depleted body that is needed in other areas of life for true transformation. Do you trust the love of God and His promises to you enough to let go of your deepest pains and fears to forgive and be forgiven by Him?

I must point out that I consider reconciliation entirely different than forgiveness—the two should not be confused. Forgiveness is letting go of an offense another has done to you. Reconciliation is something needed in a relationship when sin has separated you. Relationships require transparency and integrity from both parties. I cannot renew a relationship to the same level it once was with someone who has sinned against me if they will not repent or have the heart to reconcile. *"Let us therefore make every effort to do what leads to peace and to mutual edification"* (Romans 14:19). At this point in their walk with God, they are not in the right relationship with Him. I can release you of your offense to me, but I cannot be reconciled until you accept responsibility for your sin through repentance.

(Remember, repentance is a relational connection to Christ.) It takes humility with meekness to reconcile a damaged relationship. *"Be completely humble and gentle; be patient, bearing with one another in love"* (Ephesians 4:2). *"Love is patient, love is kind. It does not envy, it is not self-seeking, it is not easily angered, it keeps no record of wrongs... It always protects, always trusts, always hopes, always perseveres"* (1 Corinthians 13:4-7). As you come into God's perfect peace, you are then able to view the offender through the eyes of Christ with genuine compassion and forgiveness. *"Above all, love each other deeply, because love covers over a multitude of sins"* (1 Peter 4:8). *"Be kind and compassionate to one another, forgiving each other, just as in Christ God forgave you"* (Ephesians 4:32).

If you are emotionally bonded with someone who has hurt you and you feel anger, a desire for revenge, or any other negative emotion, I encourage you to continue to pray, read, meditate, and get help from a mature person in the faith to grasp His peace. Holding onto these emotions only steals the life that God has for you. *"Cast all your anxiety on him because he cares for you"* (1 Peter 5:7). Forgiveness is an intimate participation in God's grace.

When you realize your mistakes, guilt, and shame may creep in, which could prevent you from coming to Jesus. The good news is that any guilt you may experience will be corrected by receiving God's grace. And any shame will be rectified by accepting God's forgiveness. This is not a passive process; action is required to receive God's grace and accept His forgiveness.

Let me call this to your attention and leave you with these thoughts on forgiveness:

1. Forgiveness is not something Christians should take lightly. Biblically, it is not optional but a fundamental principle that guides and matures the inner self toward salvation.

2. Forgiveness is a decision of your will, motivated by your obedience to God and His command to forgive.

3. By God's grace, He forgives you, but not everyone will be reconciled to God because they do not confess and repent of their deeper emotional sins; therefore, they are not in a right relationship with Him.

4. God loves a cheerful giver, but imagine how much more He must love those who abandon themselves to His will cheerfully and completely. (A Cheerful Attitude).

WORKSTATION 7
Forgiveness—The Soul Cleanser

PRINCIPLE 1: Forgiveness releases a debt or offense. It requires that you take account of the wrong by knowing the hurt done to you and the extent of the internal damage.

Assess your situation and list your anger, rage, resentment, disrespect, and lack of forgiveness.

_____

_____

_____

_____

Now, list reasons for your pain by taking responsibility for that pain. (For example, his name-calling made you feel what):

_____

_____

_____

_____

It would be best if you kept your anger because:

_____

_____

_____

_____

PRINCIPLE 2: Do not look to your offender for renewal, restitution, or compensation. Remember, the one who caused the pain does not have the means to repay or remove the pain. It is part of your history, and only you have that control.

Your thoughts now:

_____

_____

_____

_____

PRINCIPLE 3: All anger must be released. Although anger is a normal reaction to injustice, it must be removed before freedom comes. Anger is an emotional gift from God; He is the only one you can give it back to or who can provide peace.

Your thoughts now:

_____

_____

_____

_____

PRINCIPLE 4: The offender's behavior is not essential. The integrity and sincerity of the offender are not critical for true forgiveness to be given. You do not need their specific response to be free; they are powerless.

Your thoughts now:

_____

_____

_____

_____

PRINCIPLE 5: Genuine forgiveness requires that you find compassion as a fellow sinner. You need forgiveness every day from God.

Your thoughts now:

_____

_____

_____

_____

PRINCIPLE 6: Forgiveness releases you emotionally from holding onto pain. It may not affect the person who caused the pain, but it will help balance your body's chemicals.

Your thoughts now:

_____

_____

_____

_____

PRINCIPLE 7: Although connected, forgiveness should not be confused with reconciliation.

Your thoughts now:

_____

_____

_____

_____

Just a reminder that change will not happen overnight. Therefore, you will have to revisit these principles over and over until God grants you His peace. Accepting this is also okay.

APPENDIX

A collection of mottoes and poems for further practical and mental training

RULES FOR BEING HUMAN: You will receive a body. You may like or hate it, but it will be yours for your entire lifespan. How you treat it physically, spiritually, and mentally is up to you. You are given free control.

What you make of life is up to you. You have all the internal tools and resources you need; however, your life needs to be fed and cared for with the right stuff. How that is accomplished is up to you. The choice is yours.

You will learn lessons. You are enrolled full-time in this school called Life. Each day, you will have the opportunity to learn lessons. You may like the lessons or think them irrelevant or even stupid. Nonetheless, how you internalize each lesson will affect your body and its chemistry, directly impacting your life physically, mentally, and spiritually from conception to death. The choice is yours.

There are no mistakes in this life, only lessons. These lessons can help you grow and mature. They will come in the form of trials, errors, and experiments. The failed experiments are as much a part of the process as the successful ones. You have choices.

Most lessons will be repeated in various forms until you have learned them. Skills acquired in one lesson will be needed for future lessons. Learning lessons will never end on this side of heaven. There is no segment of life that will discontinue its lessons. If you are breathing, there are lessons to be learned. They are crucial for transforming your soul to receive its new body. You make the choice.

> There is nothing better than here. However, when your there becomes your here, you will simply obtain there, which will look better than here. It would be best if you acquired the ability to live and enjoy the here and now, so your now will move you toward your eternal future. You choose.
>
> Others are merely mirrors of you. You cannot love or hate something about another person unless it reflects something you love, hate, or fear about yourself, even if you do not acknowledge or recognize it aloud.
>
> All the answers to your questions concerning your life lie within you. All you need to do is look, listen, obey, and trust your Counselor, the Holy Spirit. Because you have been so conditioned to look outside of yourself for answers and insight, you will forget all this.
>
> –ANONYMOUS

EIGHT ESSENTIAL PRINCIPLES AND

VALUES TO BE DEVELOPED INTERNALLY

FOR A SOULISH TRANSFORMATION

TRUTH—The honest expression of feelings regarding one's individualized reality. You are being honest with yourself and understanding God's truth from the heart through obedience. Be aware that truth is not made up of your opinions, likes, or dislikes.

HONESTY—A continuation of truth extending to all areas of life and character. It is an expression of truth.

HUMILITY—A modest state resulting from self-acceptance and acceptance of other people, places, and things without defensiveness or closed-mindedness. Humility enables one to share space with others comfortably and responsibly.

FORGIVENESS—A cognitive process of modifying a perception of things outside your control without judging or blaming others.

CARE—Requires a gestalt (an organized whole that is more than the sum of its parts) of the basic life principles in operation between self and others. It is goodwill toward others induced by balanced chemistry.

COMPASSION—Intensified care that brings comfort to self and others unconditionally. It is a profound sympathy, empathy, and sorrow for another person stricken by misfortune, accompanied by a powerful desire to alleviate the suffering.

ACCEPTANCE OF DIFFERENCES—The nonjudgmental ability to reconcile differences without compromising one's values. It understands the individualized realities of other people, places, and things without trying to make their reality your reality or vice versa.

GRACE—Unmerited divine assistance given to you for your regeneration and sanctification. Used as a verb, it means to do honor or credit to someone by one's presence; hence, God's presence in you. Synonyms—dignify, distinguish, honor, favor, glorify, elevate.

The changes you need involve value recognition, clarification, modification, and the proper use of your internal resources, skills, and assets. It is a true understanding of yourself concerning God's universal order of things and the principles that drive that relationship. It is living comfortably inside yourself while contributing to your well-being, that of others, and your environment. Keep in mind that life's principles and the values you live by cannot corrode, be bought, sold, lost, destroyed, or corrupted by others. You cannot destroy or abuse them without realizing the physical, emotional, or spiritual consequences. They do not lose value, but can control powerful forces within you.

TODAY

Author Unknown

This is the Beginning of a new day.

God has given you this day to use as you will. You can waste it or use it for good.

What you do today is important,

Because you are exchanging a day of your life for it.

When tomorrow comes,

This day will be gone forever,

Leaving in its place something that you have traded for it.

You want it to be gains, not losses,

Good, not evil,

Successful, not failure,

In order that you do not regret the price for it.

May you have sufficient wisdom and courage that this day shall be your record for...

TODAY!

Changing the Way You Change from ungodly beliefs should incorporate the items below, based on the Golden Rule. Can you drink this cup and not just take a few sips? And for those who see a pyramid, can you climb it with only the Bible in your hand?

Regaining hope,

Restoring yourself,

Rebuilding your life,

Picking up the pieces,

Mending broken spirits,

Raising up without fear,

Healing from past wounds,

Obtaining your self-respect,

Reclaiming your right to be,

Reviving life within and around you,

Releasing what does not belong to you,

Realizing that there is good within you,

Repossessing your mind and your heart,

Replacing them with thoughts and acts of love,

Renewing your faith, your mind, and your body,

Making amends for the spirits you have broken,

Repairing broken thoughts and faulty behaviors,

Increasing your ability to own your light and life,

Reaching out lovingly to share that light and life,

Renovating your broken dreams and broken heart,

Growing in your ability to feel the good and bad

With the ability to express both in a godly manner!

Forgive, forgive, forgive, forgive, forgive, forgive!

–AUTHOR UNKNOWN

ANALYSIS OF SELF

You have learned what you experienced, and what was learned can be unlearned with His truth and the implementation of that truth. You only need to demonstrate a behavior that shows you believe God is telling the truth. Paraphrasing Dorothy Nolte's poem, "Children Learn What They Live".

If you live with disapproval, you learn to condemn.

If you live with hostility, you learn to fight.

If you live with ridicule, you learn to be afraid.

If you live with shame, you learn to feel guilty.

If you live with tolerance, you learn to be patient.

If you live with encouragement, you learn confidence.

If you live with praise, you learn to appreciate.

If you live with fairness, you learn justice.

If you live with security, you learn to have faith.

If you live with approval, you learn to like yourself.

If you live with acceptance and friendships, you learn to find love in the world.

This poem was taken from Dorothy Law Nolte, Ph.D. (January 12, 1924–November 6, 2005), *Children Learn What They Live: Parenting to Inspire Values* (New York: Workman Publishing Company, 1998). Reworded by this author.

AN INTUITIVE ATTITUDE WORKOUT

To accomplish an Intuitive Attitude Workout, implement the following actions:

INSTRUCTIONS:

1. **READ** one question at a time and then reread that question.

2. **RELAX** by taking deep breaths through your nose, holding for 4 seconds, and then blowing out slowly for 10 seconds through your mouth. Do this at least three more times very slowly.

3. **NOW MEDITATE** in a quiet, uninterrupted place for at least 15 minutes.

4. **LISTEN TO YOUR INNER VOICE!** Normally, your authentic inner voice will not fluff you up. Be genuine and honest with yourself. Remember, being overly critical of yourself is one of Satan's ways of stopping you from becoming more Christlike.

5. **THINK!** Realize your individualized reality, be it right or wrong. Remember, you are revealing your true nature and the personality mask you have been wearing. An honest expression of your individualized reality is your only truth now, but if it is laid on a biblical foundation, conduct yourself like God is telling you the truth. However, if you question anything, measure it against the standard of truth, the 'Bible.' When you behave like God is telling you the truth, you are working on your faith and are confident that God can use you. Develop a Christlike attitude about your life.

NOTE: Discussing each question with a trusted friend may be helpful after determining your inner truths and core beliefs. Be advised that learning is only a part of the equation. You must take action, as we are told in James 2:14-26 and 1 John 3:18.

QUESTIONS FOR SELF-ANALYSIS

1. If your consciousness were a caring heart toward others, would that enhance your respect, trust, and acceptance of differences with people, places, and things that are less familiar to you?

   _____

   _____

   _____

   _____

2. Should you love one another but despise human abuse of people, places, and things?

   _____

   _____

   _____

   _____

3. Have you lost direction and serenity? Why and how?

   _____

   _____

   _____

   _____

4. Have you lost yourself in technology?

_____

_____

_____

_____

5. Are you valuing your technical gadgets over others, yourself, and God?

_____

_____

_____

_____

6. Are technical solutions the answer to your dilemma?

_____

_____

_____

_____

7. Have your attitude and behavior toward technical things polluted your social atmosphere?

_____

_____

_____

_____

8. What would be some biblical terms for this pollution?

_____

_____

_____

_____

9. Could your mental condition be a false sense of pride and serenity?

_____

_____

_____

_____

10. Could false serenity decay relationships via jealousy, envy, distrust, and competition?

_____

_____

_____

_____

11. Could so-called "little white lies" become big black clouds of rage and depression that drive you to drink, use drugs, remain in abusive relationships, or other dysfunctions?

_____

_____

_____

_____

12. Could dysfunctional coping disorders create a pecking order of individuals and groups based on your sense of superiority or inferiority?

_____

_____

_____

_____

13. Do your maladjusted conditions derive from distortive values such as lying, hiding, cheating, and stealing?

_____
_____
_____
_____

14. Have you created a dysfunctional map to plot your survival course to happiness and longevity?

_____
_____
_____
_____

15. Should you think that saving yourself within this world is the way to save the world?

_____
_____
_____
_____

16. Could your dysfunctional perceptions and induced chemistry imbalance be the root of your internal and social unrest, etc.?

_____
_____
_____
_____

ABOUT THE AUTHOR

VANESSA BRIDGES, PHD, LPC-S, has over thirty years of experience in the mental health field with a doctorate degree in Clinical Christian Counseling. She spent six months abroad in West Africa, focusing on cultural diversity.

While living in New York City, Dr. Bridges worked with CBS News under Walter Cronkite and Dan Rather. Dr. Bridges served as a program director for the local Mental Health Authority before pursuing her private practice. She has coordinated and facilitated several grassroots activities in her hometown for the empowerment of people with mental challenges. Since 1994, she has been a contract mediator for the Federal Government.

Dr. Bridges works with all adults, concentrating on family resolutions, bipolar disorders, depression, marital discord, schizophrenia disorders, and addictions of all types. Her modality is eclectic, tailored to an individual's background and needs at that time. She believes that by helping individuals integrate the knowledge and skills being presented, they will have greater success in managing symptoms and increasing their focus to reach their goals.

Dr. Bridges embodies her beliefs in learning as a lifelong process, encouraging and challenging others to continue working toward inner peace. As a creative thinker, therapist, mediator, educator, and coach, she uses her tools, insight, curiosity, experience, style, leadership, and keen interest to help others establish better possibilities from within themselves. For reviews, requests, and more, email Dr. Bridges at ctwyc.book@gmail.com.